RISKING CHANGE

Endings & Beginnings

William F. Sturner, Ph.D.

BEARLY LIMITED

Buffalo, New York

Contents

Foreword   v

Preface   vii

Introduction   ix

Precis: Looking Ahead   xi

PART I: UNDERSTANDING THE PROCESS

CHAPTER ONE   Confronting the Issues   3

CHAPTER TWO   Self-Assessment   13

CHAPTER THREE   Arenas of Change   21

CHAPTER FOUR   Basic Structures   34

CHAPTER FIVE   Principles of Risking   41

CHAPTER SIX   Dynamics of Risk   48

CHAPTER SEVEN   Process of Changing   56

PART II: FIGURING THINGS OUT

CHAPTER EIGHT   The Journeyman   67

CHAPTER NINE   Motivating Forces   73

CHAPTER TEN   The Human Clock   80

CHAPTER ELEVEN   Becoming Aware   86

CHAPTER TWELVE   Involving Others   97

CHAPTER THIRTEEN   The Four Crucial Questions   106

PART III: DOING SOMETHING ABOUT IT

CHAPTER FOURTEEN   **Knowing What to Do and When** 117

CHAPTER FIFTEEN   **Character Traits** 128

CHAPTER SIXTEEN   **Strategies for Dealing With Risk and Change** . 133

CHAPTER SEVENTEEN   **Styles of Operating** 139

CHAPTER EIGHTEEN   **Getting From Here to There** 146

CHAPTER NINETEEN   **Endings and Beginnings** 155

Suggested Reading 157

From the Publisher 161

Foreword

One of the few constants in the world is the inevitability of change. It is an issue for each of us: our interests and abilities change, our perspectives broaden, even our physical attributes can show signs of increasing maturity!

Change is also an issue faced by every nation in the world. Economic, political, and social change — these are the crucial issues confronting the policy-makers of every society and they effect the fate of individuals, institutions and entire countries.

Ireland and the United States, in particular, are no strangers to this ever-present dynamic. The citizens of our two countries have not only responded to but successfully managed a series of changes. We have, through focus and dedication, proactively created many life-giving changes as well. In the language of this book, the citizens of our two countries have wilfully and frequently taken substantial risks to achieve personal and community goals, and in so doing created life-giving changes for all humankind.

Ireland, for example, has for centuries, helped mold the political, cultural and religious institutions of major sections of the globe. It spawned such missionaries as St. Brendan and St. Columcille in the Dark Ages, and the Medical Missionaries of Mary and the Columban Fathers in recent times. It has had considerable influence on the cultural milieu through the writings of W. B. Yeats, James Joyce and Samuel Beckett, and politicians of the stature of Charles Stewart Parnell, Eamonn de Valera, and John F. Kennedy.

And, surely it was America's political Revolution, and subsequently her economic and scientific growth, which spearheaded so many changes throughout the world, and made America the risk-taking center of modern civilization.

Our two countries have become inextricably linked, allies, if you will, in a mutually beneficial relationship spanning the last three hundred years. Half of the troops who served in the American Revolution were Irish, and half of the troops serving on both sides of the

American Civil War were of Irish heritage. Eight signers of the Declaration of Independence were Irish, as were thousands who subsequently became American playwrights, entertainers, politicians and statesmen. It is the grandchildren of these pioneers who return to Ireland by the millions each year to trace the roots of their heritage.

This continuing link, this continuing cooperation, is symbolized today by the close relations that Dr. Sturner has with the offices I now supervise. It was our pleasure to have him as the keynote speaker at our Conference on Productivity in Dublin in 1986. He also has assisted the Centre in promoting change between labor and management through his frequent visits over the years. He has been, of course, well-positioned to do so, having developed a unique understanding of our two cultures while serving as Visiting Professor to our National Institute of Higher Education.

Bill Sturner is uniquely qualified to deal with the themes of risk and change. A student of both psychology and management, he has distinguished himself at every level of risk management – as a therapist working with individuals, as a consultant working with groups, and as a leader of large organizational systems.

This book is the direct result of the insights gained from these varied experiences. Most important, it is a book directed to individuals, in every walk of life, in every culture, who daily face the risks and changes involved in personal and professional growth, in social interaction, and in providing leadership to their organizations.

Life is filled with challenge. We have no choice but to face the risks involved in resolving our set of problems and fulfilling our set of opportunities. This excellent book tells us that we need not be afraid! The dynamics can be foreseen. The recurring principles are clear.

If we heed Dr. Sturner's wise counsel, then each of us – as individuals, nationals, and citizens of the world – can grow and prosper by cooperating with change. Each of us can learn to embrace the risks, however difficult, that are most essential to creating what we most desire and most deserve.

John J. Lynch
Chief Executive, Irish Productivity Centre, and
Chairman Designate of the National Employment and Training Authority
Dublin, Ireland

Preface

There are four basic theses to this book – all of which correspond to the four fundamental themes of our lives.

First, transition and change are facts of living. This is given. Careers, relationships, our sense of values, even the places where we live – take turns shedding the old and beginning the new.

Second, these transitions, although difficult and often resisted, are critical points in our development. Letting go of the old, risking to seek or accept the new, all the endings and the beginnings – are critical choice points in our development. Change, and the growth associated with it, is the moving force in our development, prodding us to become better persons, partners, and professionals.

Third, the changes in our lives – whether painful or joyful, desired or resisted, planned for or jolted into – are filled with meaning and significance. We learn that we are survivors, are durable, that we can cope, let go, and initiate. We learn that life is a process of living through and learning from the risks we take.

Fourth, in the process of changing, we become more complete human beings, maybe not at the pace and in the direction we would have preferred, but more genuinely human, capable of anger and joy, pain and celebration, affection and independence. We learn to experience the full range of feelings and activities which are the destiny and the potential of every human being.

Risk, change and the inevitable adaptation and transition they involve, prompt us into the next learning, the next cycle of the unending spiral of being true to all aspects of ourselves. Without risk and change, identities would not blossom, careers would not prosper, and our relationships would not deepen or mature.

Introduction

We all have something in common. Sooner or later, we are asked to take risks. Such invitations to grow usually happen –in big ways – several times in our lives. And, most of us need to deal with smaller changes and transitions almost daily.

Birth itself is pretty risky business, and depending on the part of the world where we are born, the risk of injury or fatality varies greatly. Even for the majority who come through that channel of life relatively unscathed, memories of that trauma lurk in the nerve cells of the body and the brain. Without consultation, we are asked to give up the gentle rocking, free meals, and the continual soaking in the membrane of warm water, and be forcefully and painfully pushed into a new world of independent breathing, suckling and groping.

As civilization has advanced, the world has witnessed a decrease, although not an elimination, of physical hardships and risks involved in obtaining sufficient food and shelter. Yet many parts of the world still suffer periodically from these risks of life. Famine, prolonged guerilla war, political oppression, and disasters caused by floods, earthquakes and hurricanes are only examples of how many still have to channel most of their life's energy into survival.

For most, however, advances in science and medicine have shifted the arenas of risk to the psychological areas of life, to risks in selecting a field of study or in launching a career; to the risks involved in courtship, marriage, parenting, divorce; to the risks in speaking our mind in a business meeting or to our mate; to the risks involved in taking a stand on our beliefs and values, or to those assumed in delving into the depths of the human psyche and the roots of one's history through therapy or counselling.

Everyone faces risk, sometimes every day. Risk arrives in multiple forms, usually when we least expect it. Whether physical or psychological, whether it involves us as individuals or as members of a family or group, whether we plan it, seek it, or it just appears without warning or preparation, risk is a constant phenomenon.

We will explore this phenomenon of risk, and the changes it involves, in various aspects of life, with an eye to uncovering practical guidelines on when and how to take risks and manage them successfully.

In particular, we will be concerned with such topics as:

1. How to embrace the need to risk, assuming the initiative in areas of our lives which need to be changed . . . whether it is personal identity and lifestyle, career development, and/or relationships.

2. How to handle situations the world sends (or that we create for ourselves), avoid the pitfalls, and manage the transitions effectively and efficiently.

3. How to tap our reservoir of skills, strengths, insights and sensitivities to make the most of a changing situation.

4. How to cooperate with change, work through resistance, deal with growing pains, and witness and celebrate our development.

5. And how, in changing, we can mature and develop, becoming, with each step, more like the person we wish to be.

Precis

Looking Ahead . . .

The process of risking change can be likened to planning a trip.

In Part I, "Understanding the Process," we will cover such analogous issues as the art of auto travelling, things to look into before you leave, a check-list of "do's and don'ts," and a list of places to visit.

In Part II, we will investigate the condition of the auto, the driver's characteristics, the cleanliness of the windshield and your glasses, the destination, and devices available for mapping the journey.

In Part III, we will complete the process by outlining options on how to handle the vehicle to insure that you reach your destination.

Part I, then, is the understanding of *WHAT* the journey of risk is about.

Part II looks more closely at the individual *WHO* will be travelling and risking.

The last section, Part III, will explore *HOW* the risker can complete the journey.

PART I. UNDERSTANDING THE PROCESS

An Examination of *WHAT* Risk Is All About

Pilgrim, there are no roads.
Roads are made by walking.

— John Manuel Serrat

CHAPTER ONE

Confronting the Issues

It was amazing to watch. It was hard to believe. The contradiction between the frailty of the body and the power of the office was so great, my mind quickly overloaded. It was one of those times when we don't know what to do with certain information, so we store it in the attic of our minds, assuming we would absorb its full impact later.

A few years later, the image was back – portrayed in the black and white of early television. The newsreel showed the President of the United States being carried to the podium of the Democratic National Convention. Two secret service men had locked arms, and after leaning over at the waist and bending at the knee, had planted their feet firmly – and waited. The President, with the help of an aide, yanked himself free from the wheel-chair, shifted his legs slightly, and leaned back into the human cradle.

Slowly the trio negotiated the four steps to the platform. Strains of "Hail to the Chief" brought the crowd to its feet and a loud roar erupted. The delegates stomped on the concrete floor and, in successive waves, picked up a series of chants that bellowed, in over-lapping cadences, across the hall. Snake dances weaved from aisle to aisle, and balloons first fell onto the throngs and then were joyfully bounced back toward the rafters. In the middle of it all, as both its cause and its reflection, was the smiling, jaunty F.D.R.

Then the booming baritone held sway. Quiet tones followed points clearly made in staccato form. Then the rise in the voice and a sentence of pronounced emphasis . . . at the end of which pandemonium erupted. The hall was so shaken the sight and sound of the speaker was momentarily lost.

Through the blur of confetti the cameras zoomed in again, and in the center of the tumult, simultaneously evoking and absorbing the wild display of energy stood the President of the United States, waving to the crowd with one hand, gripping the podium with the other.

This study in contrasts made many aware of the times we might have prematurely limped away from a challenge, fearful that we did not have the mental and physical stamina to meet it. Here was a man, obviously crippled, who despite his handicap, held the highest office in the land and was leading the war efforts of the Allied nations. He was able to move armies and nations but was unable to move his legs.

The insight provokes a set of images . . . of the risks F.D.R. had taken, personally and professionally, to establish himself as leader of his destiny, and the nation and the world. Other personalities came to mind. Helen Keller, born without the ability to speak and hear, became a writer and lecturer and the builder of schools and foundations. She had to overcome her early habits of communicating through grunts and tantrums, and risked giving up the heavy dependence on her family. Even after she made the break-through to discover the relationship between her teacher's hand signals and objects of her world, she still had to battle the ridicule and fear of the outside world as she dared to display competence and demand equality and recognition.

The world's history is filled with such transformations. Gandhi turning his back on a successful law career to be a peasant in Bombay and champion the rights of the Indian people against British rule. The Hungarian Freedom Fighters in 1956, the Civil Rights Movement in the sixties, the fight for Women's Liberation in the seventies, and in the eighties the Solidarity Movement in Poland, all exemplified the elusive qualities of courage, taking a chance and risk.

And, there are millions of average people – acting out risks which are not a part of a historic event, whose gambles are not reflected in mechanical inventions, medical breakthroughs or the founding of an organization, but whose actions demonstrate the same characteristics, the same will and ability to take a chance and thereby have a major impact on the lives of themselves and others.

These individual risks happen daily, all over the world – standing up to a bully, leaving home for the first time, building or leaving a relationship, selecting a major in college, sitting through a job interview, moving to a new town, expressing love or affection, all make a major contribution to our development. Through the ripple effect, they contribute to the growth and development of others as well.

Each of these risk-taking ventures share certain common characteristics. You will undoubtedly recognize them – for surely they have been reflected in your risk-taking ventures as well.

Think of a risky situation in which you are presently involved. Give it a one-word "label" or descriptor to help anchor it in your memory.

Now, think of a future risk, one you have longed to take, a special something which beckons to you. Give a code name or label to that potential risk. Anchor it in your memory.

Keep both your present and future risk in mind as you explore the following characteristics of successful risk-taking. Apply each to your risk behavior. Use the list as a reality check, to make sure you are on the right track.

The Ten Characteristics of Successful Risk-Taking

1. Making Choices

In successful risk-taking, there is always a need to confront a range of choices, and then to choose a course of action best fitting the situation.

You may have to choose between conflicting courses, to sell or buy, initiate or hold back, continue on as usual or set out anew. You might even have to choose between highly desired items – this house or that, this job or that, this city or that. Either way, a choice has to be made. The alternatives have to be confronted straight on. Choosing is essential in risk-taking.

2. Overcoming Resistance

Choosing among alternatives and facing the reality of

giving something up to attain something else, is often a matter of overcoming one's resistance.

First, there is the natural desire to avoid making any decision in hope that the issue will go away or that you can have the best of both possible worlds. This type of resistance has to be dealt with and overcome if risk-taking is to be more than a mental game.

Second, we have to overcome the resistance of surrendering the old to embrace the new. The old may be dysfunctional, annoying, painful – a job, relationship, or trait we never really wanted. Yet, we are used to it – and at the moment of choice, the pain of the new situation often seems so much greater than the pain of what already exists. At least we know how the present situation works, however poorly; the new situation is filled with unknowns!

3. Dis-association and Re-identification

Taking a risk entails breaking out of an existing mold. It is a deviation from the usual pattern. It creates a new and expanded boundary within which to operate. It is based on shedding an old and more restricted identity for a newer and expanded definition of oneself.

Earlier, restrictive associations must be re-negotiated or dropped. "Can't," or the assumption of inability, is first replaced by the admission of "won't, an acceptance that growth and non-growth is dependent on an act of the will. Once that is clear, new affirmations can enter our awareness. "Can do" and "will do" are integrated. The product is usually a new and more inclusive sense of identity.

Consistent with the counsel of Roberto Assagioli and his concept of "Psycho-synthesis," we can jettison the exclusivity of earlier roles and identities and add new, more inclusive ones. The internal, restrictive definitions of oneself as "mother" (and little else!), or as technician (and thus unable to venture into other areas and become "them" too!), are transformed into self-affirmations which salute one's elasticity, flexibility, and power to add to one's repertoire.

So "mother" can obviously continue as mother but once that role is no longer allowed to be confining, which is in itself a risky act of the will, then "mother" can add the abilities and identity of accountant as well! In the same way, we need to pierce the boundaries of "technician," or any other label we have for ourselves, to admit other, more-inclusive and complementary skills, outlooks and identities.

Before taking your next risk, then, be sure to check out the roles you play in life and the identifications you have assumed. Most role definitions and self-identity statements are restrictive. If you take a risk and expand your affirmations of self, or at least your sense of your potential, then you are well on your way to expanding the rest of your life and successfully achieving your risk-goals.

4. Calculated Risk

Taking a chance involves:
(1) calculation, gathering information and figuring things out as best we can beforehand, and
(2) risk, actually going to the diving board and jumping off!

We learn a great deal from calculation, from looking at our choices and clarifying our needs. At some juncture, however, we must stop and act. The rest of the information we seek can only be gained by actually entering the experience we have been contemplating. The only way to find out what it is really like to be in that new, risky situation is to actively embrace at least part of that risk. Then we will know experientially what calculations alone can never provide.

5. Gradual and Incremental Progress

Sometimes we may need to control our enthusiasm and impatience. Doing everything at once often has a lot of appeal. "If we are going to do it, then let's do it," can be a dashing approach to risk-taking, but it is also foolish. Drama at the expense of good sense is not recommended. Try to contain your excitement. Don't throw caution to the wind and attempt to revolutionize your life overnight.

A gradual and incremental process is recommended for both phases of the risk-taking process:

(1) for the analytic phase in which you gather facts, uncover patterns, and clarify both your intentions *and* your options, and

(2) for the action phase in which you implement your plans and strategies with concrete specific activities.

You don't dilute your resolve, or your action steps through gradual and incremental progress. You strengthen both. In fact, if you need to act completely and immediately without considered choice and calculated actions, it may indicate either that your resolve is very weak (i.e., you might change your mind unless you act now), or that you wish to avoid the work involved in analyzing and then pursuing your goal.

In other words, acting on your risk is essential, but so is the need for preparation, and diligently tracking what often turns out to be an elusive and moving target. A strategy of all-or-nothing avoids the work. Gradual and incremental progress is balanced. It commits to the goal and moves toward it. It simultaneously accepts and relishes the process of unfolding, the gradual and incremental process that gets us to the goal.

6. A Sense of Joy

This is not a call for simplistic positive thinking to avoid dealing with the realities of risk. We still need to confront our choices, overcome resistance, disassociate from limiting and restrictive identities, and accept the constant work needed to make incremental progress.

If we are to sustain ourselves, however, through all of this work, then "this work" called risk-taking must be seen for what it is: a joyful way of discovering who we are and who we wish to become. We don't need to adopt "a positive attitude" in lieu of a sedative or promise to help get us through the process. The process is a positive and joyful one, for it involves the discovery and application of our life energies!

Thus, the perspective of joy: "I may not be able to do everything today (for I am not God!), but I can do something today to further my evolution. And what I can do, I will do! Equally important, I will do what I can because it is me I am working on. I am the beneficiary. It is my world I am constructing. My growth and development is at stake!"

7. The Need to Decide

Taking risks is a process of making decisions. It is not just a matter of making one big decision then riding the great conveyor belt into the sky. The initial choice point – to take the leap – may be the biggest decision we face in a risk-taking process. But, there are also a series of other significant decisions which continually need to be made to support the implementation of that choice. This set of "mini-big" decisions deals with the tremendous trifles which will make or break the success of your project, all the follow-up decisions about what to do and how to do it.

Risk-taking, then, is a process of making multiple decisions. It involves one choice after another, each decision supporting the gains of others, each moving us closer and closer to our goal.

8. The Need for Focus

Once the target has been identified, and the decision "to go" has been made, once you begin to act and implement your plans, it is essential that you maintain your focus. Life is or soon gets complicated. Other problems and opportunities emerge. All the trivia of the day and week have to be attended to.

It is easy to lose one's way in the midst of this whirl of enticements, seductions and busyness. Energy can be needlessly depleted, and your focus unintentionally blurred. Thus the need

(1) to continually remind yourself of your target,

(2) to let go of the need to handle every extraneous issue

entering your life, to insure that you do not deplete your energy on less important issues,

(3) to build up your storehouse of energy by obtaining enough rest and recreation, and

(4) to focus your best and most alert energies on your risk-taking adventure.

9. Persistence, and More Persistence

It is hard to get started, and difficult to sustain the process. It is true with every risk. It may help to understand why.

Risk involves changing the pattern. That pattern initially has the upperhand, for it has history and habit on its side. Doing something to change it often feels like pushing a large stone uphill. This is why changing things feels so difficult at first. The gravity of the present pattern has enormous weight of resistance working for it. That gravity has to be overcome.

If the project goes well, and we survive this initial stage of moving a great weight (from our shoulders), then we need additional persistence to keep the process going. The feelings of going up a short, steep hill disappears, but it is soon replaced by the sense of having to complete a long journey. The persistence needed to push a large weight up a short but steep incline must now be used to work through the daily issues of perseverance.

Once the risk-goal is attained, persistence is still an issue, for the new entity must now be continuously nourished and supported to insure that the old patterns don't dilute or destroy it. The new risk now exists and has the upper hand, but until it is fixed in place through constant use and application, it still balances, at times precariously, on a teeter-totter. Without support the fulcum could shift the balance back in favor of the old pattern.

10. Issues of Control and Trust

In taking a risk, you enter into new territory. You have not been there before, or at least not in the same way. It feels

Figure 1.1 Old Ingrained Habits.

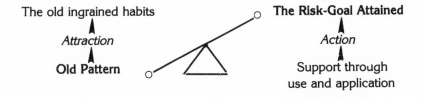

strange because it is different. It also feels strange because in entering the unknown, you have had to give up control.

Surrendering control, however, is not the same as being out of control. The skiier who skies a new area does not know what will be encountered but trusts his ability to get through it. The person doesn't know the terrain but trusts his knees to be flexible and legs to be strong. The territory is unknown but the skiier is still in control of body, pace, goal, and his ability to get down the hill.

Buckminister Fuller wrote a book entitled, *I Seem To Be A Verb.* He, the risk-taker, does not see himself to be a subject without a mission, or an object waiting to be tied into a sentence. A noun, on the other hand, may appear solid and in control but can't do anything or go anywhere on its own. The risk-taker is not a mere preposition either, or an adverb simply enhancing others.

The appropriate metaphor for the risk-taker is a verb, that aspect of language which links everything together, that alone does not have control of the meaning of the sentence, but which, by its verve and activity, controls the process of linking with whatever it needs to complete its mission.

* * *

Hopefully you have kept the theme or focus of your present risk and your next potential risk in mind as you read these characteristics of risk-taking. If you forgot, or resisted the first invitation, then you are urged (again!)

(1) to clarify those risk areas in your mind,

(2) choose a one-word label or descriptor for each, and

(3) walk them through the characteristics of successful risk-taking.

We need a reality check to compare what we are doing with what usually works. Looking at your risks in terms of the realities of the process should give you cause

(1) to affirm your skills and attitude,

(2) to give thanks for your past record of successful growth through risk-taking,

(3) to spot now – before getting too deeply into the process – any difficulties you are encountering, or ways you may be avoiding the inevitable, and

(4) to stimulate your interest in completing the next cycle of your transformation.

CHAPTER TWO

Self-Assessment

Before going any farther, let's assess our lives in terms of risk and change. Having concrete examples in mind as you read this book will enable you (1) to better apply the dynamics of risk to your experience, and (2) to anticipate what may be involved in taking the risk beckoning you.

There are three mini-lists to complete.

First, list some changes you have gone through in the **past** several years, in any area of your life.

Second, list the changes you are going through at **present.**

Third, list changes you think you will face in the **future.**

List any changes coming to mind. Try not to edit, or think of a "good" list. Just let your recollections tumble out onto the paper. Use abbreviations if you wish, letting key words like "assertive," "father," or "promotion," summarize particular events and experiences.

Past

- School
- moving
- parenthood

_____

_____

Present

- School – education
- temporary separation from spouse.
- independance.

husbands promotion

Future   *and what happens when/if*
Spouse promotion he gets it
graduation
parenthood (again)

Definition of Terms

• Change

Change occurs all the time. It is reflected in the weather, in our energy level, in the seasons, in the time of day. For some, it is also reflected in the color of our hair and need for eyeglasses. These changes occur naturally, usually without our approval.

• Risk

Risk, however, is different. Risk is chosen. It is willed. It is the result of a conscious choice. It also involves giving up something to obtain something of greater value.

Applications

1. Identifying Risks

Review the list of changes you compiled in each of the three categories and *place a check next to each item which involved taking a risk.* Risk-taking on your part could result from either your initiating that event or experience, or by re-sponding creatively to something caused by something (like the economy) or someone else (your mate or colleague, for example). Either way, risk, unlike mere change, involves a conscious and willed choice to surrender something in order to obtain an item of greater value.

2. Your Most Intriguing Future Risk

Now pick one of the items that you checked off in the future category as potentially meeting the definition of risk. Select one future risk that intrigues you the most. Risks with that much energy usually jump off the page!

The risk you choose could be the same or different from the one you selected in *Chapter One.* Circle or underline your *Most Intriguing Future Risk,* remembering it as you continue your explorations throughout this book.

Impacts of Risking

Now that you have established a record of risks you have taken, are now taking, and that you anticipate in the future, it is helpful to clarify the feelings you associate with those risk-taking experiences. In other words, based on your experience, what emotions, states of mind, and occurrences do you recall when you mention the word "risk"?

Taking inventory of your associations with risk-taking will help you anticipate the agenda of associations – both positive and negative – you inevitably bring to your next risk. That list will serve as a reminder of the issues you will confront: what concerns you have, why you may hesitate, how you get energized, what you want to do next.

Thus a set of questions to help you recall your associations. Enjoy the opportunity to set the record straight. Let your pen or pencil do the work as you jot down any feelings, reactions or associations that come to mind.

1. What happens when you *don't* risk?

— _I don't grow, I feel_
— _stagnated — things don't_
= _change — don't move on._
— _I feel as I have to_
Constantly rationalize my
decision not to risk.

Note which items are positive (+) and which are negative (−).

2. What happens when you *do* risk?

+ _I feel motivated_
+ _more experienced_
(− +) _excited and sometimes_
as I've entered a new
world

Note which items are positive (+) and which are negative (−).

3. What conclusions can you draw from the information you generated in questions 1 and 2?

I feel better about myself
and my life when I
do risk.

* * *

The Learning Cycle

The analyses of this book will enfold according to a simple learning cycle. This cycle is the same one we use unconsciously every day.

First, we will **reflect** on our life, recalling significant factors which have shaped the changes we have undergone and the risks we have taken.

Second, we will **write down** some of these recollections and reflections – jotting notes in the spaces provided, in the margin, or on separate pieces of paper.

Third, we will review the information and **discover the patterns** and themes.

Fourth, we will set or acknowledge **a new focus or goal,** one designed to grow by risking.

Fifth, we will affirm ourselves by **telling someone** else about our reflections, patterns, our new focus.

Sixth, we will support our discoveries with action, setting up a program to **do something** to attain our needs or wants.

The six steps produce a cycle which is transformed into a spiral as it acts on its discoveries and grows with each revolution. The learning process is simple but its results can be profound. Each step will help you explore and understand your life. Each will progressively deepen your commitment to working and improving your life. Together, they will help give your life more focus, setting a direction for each successive risk.

Relatively little extra work is involved in completing the cycle, for we work on these issues informally all the time. This book is only formalizing that process, making it a bit more systematic.

1. You think about your life all the time, **recalling,** experiencing and anticipating events and **reflecting** on them.
2. Gradually you become more committed, determined and better organized as you **write** some of your thoughts and intentions down.
3. You discover **patterns** which appear.
4. You pick a new **goal or focus.**

Figure 2.1   The Learning Cycle.

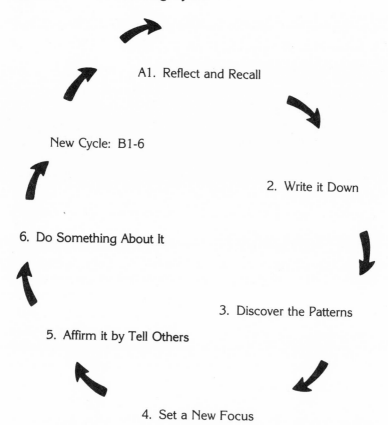

A1. Reflect and Recall

New Cycle: B1-6

2. Write it Down

6. Do Something About It

3. Discover the Patterns

5. Affirm it by Tell Others

4. Set a New Focus

5. You create momentum by **affirming** that goal to yourself and to those you trust.
6. The cycle is complete when you **do something** about it, when you undertake a set of risk activities to help you attain your goal.

Buckminister Fuller said it best: "Farming is a lot like agriculture, only farming is doing it!" The first three steps in the learning cycle – reflection, keeping a written record, and discovering the patterns and themes – are like agriculture. Setting a focus, affirming your intentions, and then doing something about them, is akin to farming.

It would be foolish to farm without information on modern agricultural techniques. On the other hand, anyone who does not support analysis with action, or get behind the plow and plant new seeds in new ways, is forever condemned to knowing but not doing, to thinking but not growing.

Ground Rules

You may want to keep the following Ground Rules in mind as you apply this learning cycle to your risk-taking.

1. Clues.

There are no quick and dirty answers. There are only clues. You have spent many years becoming who you are. That unique set of experiences cannot be unravelled in ten minutes. The essential building blocks are the clues you accumulate as you read and apply the points in each chapter.

As you accumulate enough clues, you will see the patterns. It is like filling in a dot-to-dot book. Slowly but surely, the picture of the rabbit – or the "turkey" – appears. Each dot is crucial. Each clue reveals something about the pattern, the emerging focus, and the potential set of activities which will help you attain your next risk.

It is like playing Sherlock Holmes, Father Brown or Columbo. You are both the investigator and the investigated. You can gather all the facts and make a marvelous deduction like Holmes. You can play your hunch like Father Brown. You can go over the same territory again and again like Columbo until the obvious suddenly appears.

You can even invent your own style of problem-solving and risk-taking. Whatever your approach, notice how you and your intentions will appear more clearly with each clue – like a photographic negative emerging in the developer. Assume that your risk-taking adventure will feature YOU as a unique entity, applying your special skills, in your preferred setting, to attain your most-desired goal.

2. Expertise is in You

The most essential information, and ability to analyze it, is already lodged within you. Nobody knows you better than you do. Nobody else has your storage of information about you – your patterns, intentions, and needs. You are now or potentially an expert on yourself!

3. Work at Your Pace

Everyone works at a particular pace. Choose the one best for you – taking whatever time you need to read, absorb and apply the learnings of each chapter. There is no recommended pace. Trust the one that feels right to you!

4. Take Good Care of Yourself

Make the book work for you. Take breaks whenever you want – even in the middle of chapters! Take time off between each chapter, as necessary, allowing time for absorption through incubation.

5. Enjoy Forming Your Future

As you will see in the chapters dealing with strategies and style, it is best to approach risk-taking with a balance of both analysis and action. Neither can be forced or rushed, and combining them successfully takes patience.

It is essential, therefore, that you learn to trust yourself. Have fun with risk-taking. Try not to rush head-long into the future and miss the process of encountering yourself. Apply the old saying: "Happiness is not a station in life. It is a way of travelling." So relax. Enjoy yourself and your process of risking change. Tell your friends. Affirm yourself. Have some ice cream. Enjoy!

CHAPTER THREE

Arenas of Change

There are three major areas of risk-taking. The first is personal, dealing with those crucial issues of self-identity, confidence,
esteem and acting in accordance with our values.

The second is social, including the interactions we have with
our mate, children, parents and friends. The issues here usually
are related to giving and receiving, and to maintaining one's
identity, while sharing a larger identity as a member of a twosome
or a larger group.

The third is professional, involving what we do to maintain
a sense of professional identity and competence. For instance,
we make choices about what to study, where to apply for jobs,
how to learn what's happening at the office, and how to get
someone's attention and approval for a promotion or a raise.
During these activities, we play out our risks around identity and
competence with such people as instructors, trainers, interview-
ers, supervisors, colleagues and subordinates.

Each of these arenas has many external, tangible aspects
to them – like the financial risks taken in purchasing a stereo for
your enjoyment (personal), a new piece of equipment to help in
your job (professional), or your home (social). Such risks around
the acquisition of "things" are significant, but are only the tip of
the iceberg. Our attention here will be on the much larger seg-
ment below the surface, on the causal factors which lead to a
purchase or other activity.

This book will focus, on our internal dynamics, on how we
grapple with hesitation and fear. In the case of a large purchase,
we may have to work through our lack of confidence in ourselves
("I never made such a large purchase before") or the unsettled
nature of our future earning power. These are the underpinnings
of risk which must be dealt with before completing the act of
buying anything. It is the emotional-psychological experience of

risk which needs to be worked through. Once that has been resolved, the rest is relatively easy.

Personal

This is the most basic and the toughest, for here we must take a part of ourselves, and ask "it" and get "it" to bend or change. This is the ultimate battleground, where old habits and engrained ways of operating fight for their lives.

Personality traits which may once have been helpful, getting us through difficult times, may in changed circumstances be roadblocks to effectiveness and personal growth. Learning to say "no" at age two is helpful in developing an independent ego, but if not governed by other ways of handling diverse situations could produce a chronic case of stubbornness and crankiness.

On the other hand, being diplomatic in board meetings for twenty years is not necessarily training for straight-forward expressions of love and affection with your mate or children. Being first in every race you ever entered is not always an advantage in learning to set a model for give-and-take in complex situations.

Being quiet and demure can be an endearing trait but not in an employment interview. Being outspoken can be an advantage in some situations but not in a delicate labor-management negotiation or settling a neighborhood dispute – both of which may involve someone taking a risk on behalf of compromise, mutual respect, and listening to others.

Learning repertoire and when to apply which skill or ability or facet of our personality is difficult, challenging and risky. It demands continually placing ourselves in the position of being a "learner" and not a "knower". Flexibility, not always having our way, giving and taking, confronting our fears and foibles – and doing it of our own volition because we sense the call to personal growth – are the hallmarks of the risking change process.

Changing others and getting organizations to bend, guiding our children, leading our colleagues, and being diplomatic with our supervisors, are nothing in comparison to confronting ourselves and assuming a willingness to respond to one more turn of our personal evolution.

Giving up a habit, an unquestioned assumption, a childhood fantasy, or an adult dream, muting our greatest ability on behalf of developing the opposite side of ourselves, deciding to climb out of the velvet rut on behalf of "something" whose future is nebulous and where the rewards are unclear – all this shedding of the former self to accept a challenge from some inner wisdom which beckons us to develop and embrace a new turn of the spiral – this is the arena of risk incarnate.

Social

Our social interactions are primarily focused on our significant others. This is the arena of relationships – with our mate, children, parents, and friends.

1. Romance

The central issue in romance is overcoming our insecurities to connect with another, and overcoming our fears to connect in love with another.

Asking for a date, saying "yes" or "no" to an invitation, giving up time with friends to cultivate a relationship with someone special – force us to confront tough issues. Then there are the tasks of moving to the next stage of sexual and emotional intimacy, and of setting boundaries on what we do and don't want in a relationship.

Other lessons, if we learn how to take the risk, include learning how to renegotiate an implied "contract" or understanding; moving closer to commitment or obeying a need to leave a relationship, and becoming clear by stating our needs versus letting them fester inside indefinitely.

Each of these issues is loaded with nuances only the individual experiencing them can clearly identify. In each case, the risks involve identifying what we want and need, figuring out how to get it and then taking the bigger risk of doing something about it.

2. Children

We have all been there, and some of us carry the scars of childhood all our lives, if the lesson of separate but interdependent identities was not resolved in the early years. Fortunately, many survive the traumas of childhood with honor, allowing them to nourish the joy of being child-like throughout our lives.

The lessons of childhood, much like the other categories summarized here, can be noticed by reflecting on our childhood, or the childhood of our children, or by just relating to the kids in the neighborhood.

Children need care and most parents respond to those needs. Yet, there is a need to revise the dependency link as children grow older. They need to learn to clean their room, do chores, and assume responsibility. Most parents, weary of the years of cleaning up after the little urchin, are more than ready to excite some self-responsibility in their growing child. But how much self-responsibility is too much is another matter, for with it comes the child's urge for freedom. Then the parents and the child face the dilemmas of working out the boundaries.

The risks are always great. With each pull and tug by the parent, and each ambivalent urge for more freedom by the child to seek an as-yet-unclear identity, comes the price of surrendering the familiarity and comfort of the earlier but outworn way of operating for an unknown, unpredictable future.

3. Parents

The risks involved in working with our parents are as great as any other area. They involve the risks to speak or hold our tongue, and include the expression or holding back of love and tenderness. They become decisions involving the expression of differences and the need for clearer boundaries between personalities.

The biggest risk in working with our parents is finding a balance between these alternates of affection and differences.

The situation is the same as when we were young, only now the roles often are reversed, with the nagger now becoming the naggee.

It is relatively easy in most relationships with parents to be consistently accepting or confronting, giving way at the expense of your needs or just rolling over the opposition. How to both honor the other and yourself, and to do so with appropriate doses of love and assertiveness, as the situation demands, is truly the mark of the risk taker.

4. Friends

With friends it is different. It is not easy but it all seems easier. One of the most difficult things for anyone to learn is how to apply the dynamics of friendship to loveship. In fact, we all seem to spend considerable time in friendships consoling each other about the poor communication and difficulties we are having with our mates and families. With friends there is much less guilt, fewer sets of "should's," and hardly any sticky lamentations about neglect and breaking somebody's heart. In friendships, there is more acceptance of the other as they are. In fact, the uniqueness of the other is usually valued in a friendship while in a family the "different one" is usually scorned as the trouble-maker!

Friendships evolve in levels of closeness, and both parties are usually free to pursue a frequency and level of interchange best for each.

The nice thing is that you don't have to love someone in a friendship, you just have to like them. With families it is often the reverse. You may not like your uncle, sister or parent — and that is okay — but there is some invisible edict commanding that you "love" them, making the system susceptible to all sorts of guilt trips and blurred identities. Blood is thicker than water, but water is clearer and cleaner. Water also evaporates faster, but only when the climate gives it reason. Families, God love them, will be here forever, but why, many lament, can't they be more like friendships?

Lofty intentions are easier to recite than to live by, making friendships a training ground for other social arenas. The exchange of support can often be more important than a wide array of common interests for at least someone is available to listen to our woes and tribulations. And, there are instances of having a lot in common—interest in the theatre, football, or the opposite sex—yet feeling left out when it comes time for the other to make a little sacrifice and just be there for us.

This is another case of the need to define who we are and what we want, deciding whether the price of time, energy and sometimes money, is worth the return in solace, affirmation, and valuing the same things.

Professional

Our professional interactions span many roles. There are bosses and supervisors, colleagues, subordinates, and given the hierarchical system in most organizations, considerable variation in how we interact with others. The more elevated the role and the farther it is from us on the organizational chart, the more formal and non-contactful the relationship. The closer that "other" is in organizational standing, the greater the potential for the interaction being informal, friendly and interdependent.

Unlike families, professional relationships are driven by granting a service in exchange for compensation. That contract can be broken by either party at almost any time. Since love does not enter into it, neither does guilt. Unlike friendships, the exchange is formal; you may not like a person but you have to work with them.

Working with or for someone may be loaded with legal expectations but rarely with emotional obligations. Working in the same office is not the same as living under the same roof or really needing to like the other.

Yet a lot of our hopes and dreams—for money, promotion, recognition, career development, self-worth, and even a sense of identity—depend on cooperation with these professional acquaintances. Most of the time it calls for a highly flexible weaving in and out of tight situations. Risk is involved.

The highest risks seem to come in confronting the boss for a raise or promotion; a colleague for non-support at a critical junction; a subordinate for not doing the job. If we already have a reputation for direct talk – a rarity in most organizations (for that's exactly what threatens people and procedures the most) – then our biggest risk is in doing what may come easy to others: walking away, compromising, or pouring soothing syrup over a troubled situation.

For some it is equally stressful to ask co-workers for help, reprimand a subordinate, speak up in a meeting, say "no" to one more assignment, or raise questions about a policy everyone has endorsed.

Risking in a professional setting focuses on two issues. One involves a situation in which the risker desires something and decides to do something about it, and in doing so deviates from their usual behavior. This is as risky for organizations as for the risker. Neither like to depart from established patterns. Leaving the normal groove is also very risky for the single entrepreneur or free-lancer, for he or she enters the unknown without much to fall back on, or an organization in which to recoup or hide.

The other issue involves either doing too little or too much. Too little and we miss the boat. Too much and we sink it. Which strategy is required is not always clear. Thus the risk.

*   *   *

Since our energies are divided between these three major arenas, it might be helpful to look at each in comparison to the other two. In other words, how much time and attention do you now devote to each arena? How is the energy in one arena related to that devoted to the others? Assuming you can change the proportion of energy devoted to each, how would you prefer to divide your time and attention?

The best way to give ourselves quick feed-back on both our present and preferred behavior is to draw a few diagrams. In the illustrations below, the use of energy in the **Present Situation** (for a fictitious individual) reveals primary devotion to professional interests, little attention to personal issues, and only slightly higher energy given to social-relationships. None of the arenas are connected or even close to each other; each has separate and strong boundaries. The life of the person portrayed is clearly segmented, and perhaps is experienced as fragmented.

On the other hand, the diagram of the **Preferred Situation** reveals several marked changes. Notice that the time and attention devoted to Professional needs has shrunk considerably, the energy devoted to Personal is now the largest, and that interest in Social-Relationships has increased as well.

Figure 3.1

The Present Situation (Illustrative)

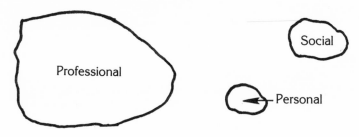

The Preferred Situation (Illustrative)

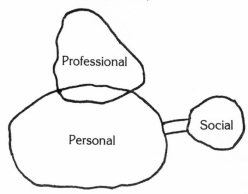

The relation between one arena and the other has also been altered. The diagram of the Present depicted strict separation. This new Preferred diagram shows a connection between Personal and Social, and an overlapping between Personal and Professional, suggesting a desire for more and better integration of one's life.

YOUR DIAGRAMS

Remember that the diagrams above are illustrative. Don't model your life or your drawings on them! Let your pencil tell your own story of how you presently devote your energy among the three arenas, and how you would prefer to spend your time and attention.

Use the spaces provided, and draw your diagrams of your Present Situation and your Preferred Situation.

My Present Situation

My Preferred Situation

CONCLUSIONS

Now interpret your diagrams, filling in your response to the following questions:

Present Situation

What conclusions can I reach about my diagram of the Present?

My Social / family
relationships take up a
majority of my energy.
Although they are all
tied together.

What is dominant or relatively neglected?

Social dominant
personal Somewhat
neglected.

What relationship does one arena have to another?

They are connected
and inter related.

What feels right or easy, and what feels tense or out of whack?

The social relationship feels right.
The lack of personal feels tense

Preferred Situation

What conclusions can I reach about my diagram of the Preferred?

All relationships are balanced and intertwined

What is dominant or relatively neglected?

none

What relationship does one arena have to another?

all related about the same amount.

_____

_____

_____

What feels right or easy, and what feels tense or out of whack?

Maybe personal shouldn't
be so large.

_____

_____

_____

Recommendations to Myself

The diagrams of my Present and Preferred Situations suggest that I investigate the following options, or do the following things:

1. _Put more energy into personal arena_

2. _less balance social and professional_

3. _____

_____

4. _____

_____

5. _____

_____

REVIEW

In *Chapter Two: Self-Assessment,* you were asked to list past changes you experienced, the ones you were going through at present, and those you anticipated or hoped for in the future.

You were then asked to determine which were really risks – that is consciously and deliberately chosen or willed.

1. Is there any relationship between the items you listed earlier as **Past and Present Risks** and your diagram, above, of your **Present Situation?** *yes all social risks*

2. Is there any relationship between the items you listed earlier as **Future Risks** and the diagram you drew of your **Preferred Situation?** *Future risks are social although more proffessional*

3. Is there any particular relationship between the **Most Intriguing Future Risk** you circled or underlined in *Chapter Two: Self-Assessment,* and your diagram of your **Preferred Situation?**

Yes, involves more personal social + proffessional risk. and relationships.

CHAPTER FOUR

Basic Structures

Three basic structures are involved in the risk-taking process. The first focuses on Personal Responsibility. The second is concerned with the Extent of Change. The third deals with Complementary Energies. Each is crucial to understanding our role in risk-taking.

1. Personal Responsibility

Taking a risk is serious and often difficult business. By definition, we must initiate, take a stand, face a possible loss, work hard, and assume responsibility for our wishes and actions. It is often easier to wait until someone else takes a risk and changes our situation to accommodate our secret desires.

Thus, we often delay acting in the hope that others will assume the responsibility to act on their behalf and thus indirectly serve our needs. We thereby are spared the work-load, avoid possible grief, and circumvent the risk-taking process.

This philosophy can often make us impatient and demanding. Blame is assessed and accusations follow. We usually start with the most nebulous and complex of the forces. "If only the culture of this _____ (city, region, country) was different, things would be all right!" we argue. Culture can mean anything from "people in general," or "the mores of our society," to the "younger generation," or "the state of the economy." Whatever it is, IT is far away, hard to define, difficult to change and surely at fault!

With a modicum of humility we turn our wrath on the organization at-large. If only the ways things work around here were different, we would not be in a fix or deprived of what we want or need." This slightly more identifiable demon is not as all-encompassing as the culture, yet the dynamic is the same: We still project blame and responsibility for action on someone or something other than ourselves.

The next level of de-escalation points a finger at particular policies or procedures "which obviously are at fault." Failing to prod changes there, we accuse a particular group of inactivity, whoever they may be: the leaders, the people in personnel, or our in-laws! If only they would change, if only they would grab the reigns of power and responsibility and institute the necessary changes, then you and I would be all right!

Figure 4.1   Personal Responsibility.

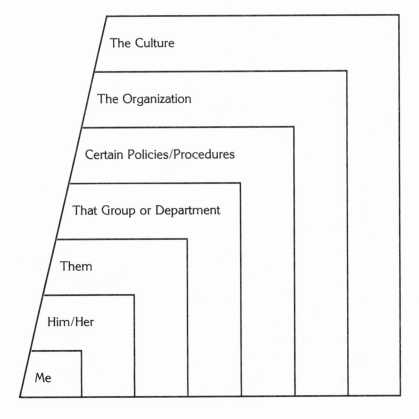

As you can see from the diagram on "Personal Responsibility," the core of the process, the central agent in the risk-taking process, is the individual complainer and risk-shirker. "Me-Myself" is at the bottom of the process, although we may not realize it. We obviously still have "them" — whoever they may be — to alternately blame and encourage. "Those who control the money," or "that clique setting the agenda for our family, department or city," are obviously the ones who should act!

The last but not the least of our deflections from personal responsibility is to bemoan the inactivity of somebody in particular. "If only Big Louie or Mildred would get their act together," we reason, "then things would be just fine. Better yet, why don't they stop crying and delaying, assume responsibility, and get on with it!" This is the last of the deceptions which assume that life would be so much more exciting and rewarding, if only someone or something else assumed total responsibility and thereby relieved us of our own!

If and when we finally get to the illusive "Me," we reach the core of the issue. Even though the culture, the organization, rules and regulations, the group, them, and him or her, may all share in creating or perpetuating a problem, and even though these outside forces may share responsibility for not seizing on a particular opportunity, the central issue in the risk-taking process is the need to assume responsibility for one's life and for any risks needed to change it.

The forces at the higher reaches of the hierarchy can and do impact greatly on those below, and power to influence the forces above us decreases considerably as we descend the ladder. Yet, impact ripples both up and down. "Me" is often the only starting place I have. It certainly is the place where I can exert the most direct control!

Inaction because others have not taken care of our needs is a sure sign of self-denial, self-surrender, and dis-empowerment; waiting for him, her or them to act on our behalf is to deny the power and the responsibility we already possess.

Besides, most of the changes we seek – to attain our personal, professional, and social needs – don't really involve most factors on the ladder. We use our accusations of "their" alleged inactivity and negative power as a cover-up or scapegoat for our hesitation, our fear, our inability to take risks, in our arenas.

2. The Extent of Change

As we overcome the tendency to delay personal responsibility in favor of watching others work – in the hope of getting "them" to commit their energies on our behalf – we then face the issue of deciding on how much change we should risk.

Having finally reached the brink of action, there is a tendency to assume that the bigger the risk the better. After all, an all-or-nothing attitude is best if we have to muster personal responsibility, analyze the options, and then adopt a course of action. If that is the case, then we might as well make a big and complete show of it; it's at least efficient, given all the time and energy to be expended!

But there is a danger here. As demonstrated in **Figure 4.1** on the next page, total, extensive or multiple changes can leave us without any mooring. All change and no conservation (point A) can easily create fragmentation.

The opposite, or point C, where change is overruled by the need for preservation, is equally dangerous. This end of the continuum can stymie change to such an extent that it enshrines the status quo, guarantees entrenchment, and fosters a feeling of suffocation. Such a bunker-house mentality brings quietude but little growth.

The greatest potential lies in the middle ground of point B – in the varied proportions or mixtures of change and preservation, in embracing risk in one area while maintaining continuity in others. Not only are the extremes of fragmentation and suffocation avoided, but the middle ground will keep our focus on specifically targeted goals, taking measured risks in specific areas while holding other elements constant.

Figure 4.1   The Extent of Change.

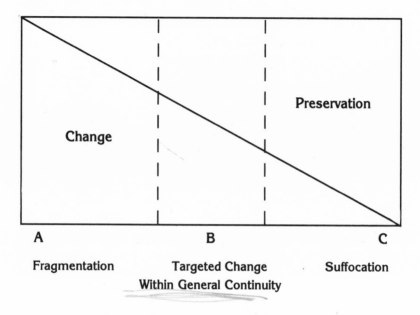

In other words, it is best not to change all your relation-ships or anything else in your life at the same time. It is also not a good idea to renegotiate a relationship, change jobs or careers, and reform your personal values or ways of operating in the same week-end! One risk will surely have an impact on other areas – and that may present its own problems. Keep-ing a possible ripple-effect under control, however, is much easier than deliberately putting everything up for grabs all at once.

3. Complementary Energies

If personal responsibility has been assumed and personal power acknowledged, and if the extremes of all change versus no change are avoided in favor of a targeted risk balanced by relative peace and quiet in rest of one's life, then you are ready to activate the flow of risk-taking energies.

Figure 4.2   The Complementary Energies of Risk-Taking.

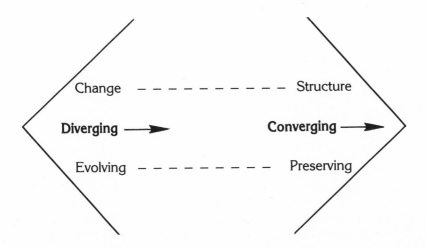

Two complementary processes must be embraced and combined if risk-taking is to be successful. They are first, diverging energy, and second, converging energy. As displayed in the above diagram, "The Complementary Energies of Risk-Taking," the energy of diverging opens up the possibilities. It massages the existing pattern by looking at options. It is exploratory in nature. It is an attitude or perspective that wishes to improve or perfect the present situation by changing it. It is the energy of evolving and moving on, of the spiral groping for one more turn of the wheel.

Once the diverging energy spots the target of change and deliberately takes a risk to change that situation, the new change needs the complementary energy of converging to protect it. As the risk is adopted and the desired change is attained, a new structure has to be built around it to solidify the gains and preserve the newly emerging relationship, career or way of operating.

Diverging opens up the old structure and takes a course of action to attain a targeted goal. Converging brings structure to the new entity and preserves it – until such time as the will to risk activates another round of diverging energy.

*   *   *

Successful risk-taking, then, involves several different skills and abilities.

We must be willing to accept responsibility for our lives, and to use whatever power or control we have to bring about the changes we desire.

We need to consider the advantages of balancing risk and change in particular areas while maintaining continuity in others.

And when we act, we would be wise to anticipate the need to muster sufficient diverging ability to open the old situation to new possibilities. Having made the changes created by our risk, we need to invoke our skills in converging, supplying energy to protect the new creation with a nourishing structure of its own.

CHAPTER FIVE

Principles of Risking

The process of risking is a cumulative one. Understanding each dynamic allows you to grapple with and master the next one. What is intended is not just that you read the twenty-five principles governing the risking process, but that you internalize their message so the principle is ingrained in your process.

The ability to internalize a "truism" so it affects your behavior depends on having a dialogue with it — creating a conversation within yourself about how to use the insight. For example, you might try some of the following approaches.

Apply the Principle to Your Life

Ask such questions as, "If I had known this, how would I have avoided a mistake I made," or "What would I have done differently?"

Second, apply the principles to current issues. Try giving yourself concrete illustrations about how a principle could help you now.

Personalize the Applications by Keeping Notes

Underline or highlight key phrases in this book. Make notes to help you to go beyond intellectual understanding. Try to convert the principles into working truisms with practical applications for present and future actions.

Say the Principle Aloud as an Affirmation

Convert the principle into an "I" statement and say it aloud. You could convert principle one into an affirmation sounding like: "I grow and develop through risk. I will become a more complete, mature human being by taking risks. My life is and will become a successive series of ever-expanding risks."

Visualize Yourself Successfully Completing a Risk by Applying the Principle to That Situation

Having a picture of yourself in mind as a concrete illustration of successful risk-taking will help you build greater confidence in approaching the risk. The more specific you can become in seeing the details – what you are doing, who else is involved, how others react to you, the setting and the things around you – the greater the chance of your realizing your goal. Visualizing a constructive outcome, will help you act according to those images and thereby create the activities you envision.

These suggestions can help make your reading more vivid and have you think about constructive applications. If you have other ways of translating the material into concrete applications, as you read, then by all means use them instead. But, find a way to think more deeply about the material, creating mental applications to help it work for you.

The principles are presented progressively, as continuing points of growth on a continuum, or as increasing levels of effectiveness filling a column of energy. Visualize each as adding to the upward flow of a bar graph or the chart of a fund-raising campaign.

Each principle stands on the shoulders of the one before. Each as internalized by you, adds to your process of unfolding. Each, as applied by you, moves you closer to effective risk-taking. Living according to Principle 25, then, is akin to yelling "Bingo!"

Many of the principles outlined are covered elsewhere in greater depth. Their headline versions are amassed here in order to display their connectedness and their cumulative impact.

The Principles.

1. Everyone grows and develops through the dynamics of risk. Each of us become a more complete human being by taking periodic risks. Life is nothing but a successive series of ever-expanding risks.

*   *   *

2. Risking is the essential psychic investment in our future. When we cultivate an attitude that wishes to embrace risk as a process, we further our development. When we resist without reason, we erect obstacles to our growth.

* * *

3. Risk involves changes and transitions, transitions to expanding views of ourselves.

* * *

4. Risk involves giving something up to get something new.

* * *

5. Taking a risk means embracing the unknown and dealing with the fear of giving up control.

* * *

6. We can take risks involving tangible things, like money, to obtain other tangible things, such as a house. We can also take risks with intangible factors, such as emotion, to attain other intangibles such as love in relationship with another person.

* * *

7. The risk you are thinking about or will soon contemplate is not your first risk. Everyone's history is studded with risks. It is vital to recall all the risks we have taken, to reaffirm your successes, and to review the behavior which made each risk successful. This will insure confidence the next time a risk beckons.

* * *

8. Risking is a learned behavior, and the best way to develop it is to take risks, small ones at first, building up to larger ones.

* * *

9. The results of taking risks can be good, bad or indifferent — and at times wonderful or calamitous. Just because something feels risky does not mean you should do it. Weighing the alternatives and anticipating outcomes is what we call "calculated risk," which is quite different from blind or impul-

sive behavior. Calculated risk – "yes"; silly larks and compulsions to act quickly no matter what – "no"!

* * *

10. Not all risk involves an either/or decision, a total giving up of the past to embrace the future. Sometimes the greatest risk is in integrating parts of the old with elements of the new. The proportional mix of old and new, and the speed and degree by which we let go and add on, is called pacing.

"Pacing" will differ from one person to another. It will even vary from decision to decision for the same person. The important thing to know is the pacing needed for the decision or risk contemplated.

* * *

11. The key to including an appropriate dose of risk in our lives and at a pace in sync with our needs, is to learn more about our personality style and the risk strategies accompanying it.

* * *

12. Each of us has a personality, a cluster of beliefs, values and ways of operating, which form a perspective through which we select and organize the information guiding our decisions. This perspective is molded by a combination of factors including physical attributes and early socialization in our upbringing. All our experiences condition our values and ways of operating and therefore have an impact on our personality.

* * *

13. Although no longer as impressionable now as we were in our formative years, our personalities are still being formed or completed. Thus, changes in how we operate are still taking place.

* * *

14. The dynamic which accounts for our continuing development is our risk-taking style. It is one of the most important aspects of our personalities, and one by which we continue to evolve, change, and grow. It is the inner drive by which we perfect the process of our development. This aspect of

ourselves continually seeks to be more complex and varied, adding to our repertoire an ever-widening array of abilities and ways of interacting with the world.

*   *   *

15. Our risk-taking style is activated by two competing forces. Together they account for the rate and types of change we incorporate into our lives.

    One force is the urge to preserve, structure, to nurture the present and to live according to a patterned way of doing things. Its attributes are structure, harmony, predictability, minimal change, maximum security, peace and quiet.

    The other is the will to evolve – an inner drive to perfect the process of growth and development. Its attributes are change, risk, letting go of old structures and letting in new behavior traits.

    Both needs – to preserve and to change – are essential. Life needs change and adaptation to grow and survive. It also requires the ability to surround change with nourishment and structure, to preserve the new form so it is not easily washed away.

*   *   *

16. Which factor – preservation or change – is dominant at any time varies from person to person, situation to situation. But, there is a central paradox which makes life difficult. We all want to preserve the best and change the rest. Which is which is not always clear.

*   *   *

17. Changing every aspect of our lives at once is death through fragmentation and disintegration. Preservation of everything at once is death through stagnation. The best strategy is to select some area for change while holding others constant.

    The process of selection is similar to the scientist who tinkers with a definable aspect of an experiment, localizes the change and increasing the range and amounts of change in calculated, definable measures. The human psyche is somewhat more complicated than this since it is harder to keep one change from affecting other aspects of life. Yet the analogy is helpful: It is best to change "this" while preserving "that," and to increase the dosage of change with caution and prudence. The strategy counsels for a gradual and ever-widening change versus immediate, wholesale change.

*   *   *

18. A few ironies occur with risk-taking. One is that we may wish to change something without giving up anything, a sort of a "have your cake and eat it too" approach. This is difficult to do with material things since few dealers will let you have a car for nothing. In the intangible area of emotions and relationships, if we don't give up anything, we grow psychologically obese. With each layer of cumulative "fat," we become more bloated, progressively losing our vitality and ability to move.

*   *   *

19. We also should be careful of the "on again, off again" syndrome, like the thermostat which turns off the heat at 72 degrees and starts it again at 71. It is the irony of the double message – inviting changes in such tiny increments that they are self-defeating – for each step forward is countered by another step backward.

This method of operating allows us to feel "busy" – like we are doing a lot – while in truth we are never really pursuing a goal long enough to allow anything to happen. This "feint and retreat" approach creates what Gestalt psychology calls "unfinished business," what physicians diagnose as "constipated," or what the plumber knows as "clogged."

*   *   *

20. Most of us have a 60-40 division of energies: 60 in favor of leaving things alone, and 40 ready to change things.

Altering this 60-40 division usually depends on one of several factors: On the slow accumulation of pressure which compounds a situation and nudges us to do something about it; on cumulative and intense pain; on sudden and sometimes complete shocks, throwing current patterns into disarray, making our personalities more willing to embrace goals and activities which would have been impossible otherwise; or, on the strong desire to heed an internal beckoning to take a constructive risk we know we must take to grow and develop.

* * *

21. There are several fundamental ways of avoiding risk. By recalling past events and monitoring present ones, you can identify your special way of blocking or avoiding your own growth.

* * *

22. Once you know how you avoid taking risks, then you can use a set of techniques (most of which you can and will design yourself) to break down your avoidance behavior, embrace the appropriate risk behavior, and move ahead in your own development.

* * *

23. Proactive risk for a constructive purpose is the engine the personality uses to develop. Proactive and constructive risk is the handmaiden of invention, of growing repertoire, of new goals taking us beyond past accomplishments and spurring us to new insights, vistas, and identities.

* * *

24. Once you more thoroughly investigate the possibilities of the proactive constructive risks that have been rummaging through your mind and your gut, then you can devise a series of risk strategies for furthering your own development.

* * *

25. Risk behavior is the unending dynamic of living. The more you know about it, the more you can guide your development through constructive and creative activities. Your life will be enlivened and energized by proactive risk. It can become like an ever-widening concentric circle, known to the gods as a spiral.

CHAPTER SIX

Dynamics of Risk

The process of risking works in definable ways. Outlining it is relatively easy, but the experience itself is much more difficult.

1. We know we are about to risk when we hesitate and resist.

When something catches our attention, and simultaneously generates a bit of fear, we know we are in the territory of risk. The beckoning of something new will, of necessity, involve giving something up to get it. That's when the difficult part starts.

The exchange could involve getting a new car and surrendering the money to buy it. In the same way, asking for more freedom or space in a relationship can involve the risk of breaking the connection completely – either by the other's reaction or by your capacity for centrifugal force, given the new momentum of "moving away." Conversely, moving closer in a relationship entails giving up some of the freedom associated with single life.

As we add new abilities to our ways of interacting with others – such as expressing affection or confronting a behavior we don't like – we will have to surrender some of our shell or the wimpishness of never setting boundaries. Either way there is a loss and a gain involved. The sense of gain beckons us. The sense of potential loss causes hesitation and resistance.

Dealing with internal resistance is more difficult than a simple arm wrestle with a friend. It may feel like arm wrestling – like an external power trying to overcome us – but the resisting culprit is ourself. The struggle is internal, and the combatants are the ingrained versus the emerging parts of our personality.

Saving money rather than spending it on the car, or acting a certain way in a relationship, or always being in control of one's emotions versus showing affection naturally, opting to avoid rather than confront somebody – these ingrained traits will fight for their lives if we try to push them aside. The fear of being displaced produces resistance, a feeling which can be ignited by a tangible item existing outside ourselves (such as spending money for a new car) which triggers an intangible trait inside us (like the sub-personality of always being a good saver rather than a spender).

When an opportunity appears, it generates the defense by the old dominant characteristic, and the see-saw begins, with beckoning and opportunity on one side and hesitation and resistance on the other.

2. Risk is a "call to adventure," the cutting edge of all growth.

The process of risking is like a spiral, and riskers want to exceed themselves, making a wider arc with each cycle, passing things accomplished in the previous revolution.

Compare this to the workings of a circle. Those who live as if they were revolving in the same circle, are usually in motion but always in the same orbit, cutting, inevitably, a deeper groove in the same repetitive pattern, getting more and more comfortable in their rut, never changing course or risking to go out on an unknown orbit. There is a lot of busy-ness but no growth. It highlights comfort, ease and quietude, all within the recurring cycle.

There are others who live like a square. A square is solid, with clear boundaries separating it from the rest of the world. It does not revolve, and has four equal sides. Like the circle, nothing gets in or out. No ruts here – for not even the present is repeated – but there is the potential for not moving at all. The square personifies the line from Rudyard Kipling: "The standing army stood."

There are parabola-people who fly into space and some polygon-folk who have so many sides they are unsure which is which. People who resemble a triangle can be solidly placed or set precariously off-balance, depending on the length of the sides or how it is tilted.

Growth and development, alas, belong to the spiral. It has a history in its prior revolutions – a sense of presence in the direction of its vector or pointer. It has layers of strength. By definition it can go beyond itself, and it can grow, following its cutting edge into the future.

Human Traits Symbolized in Geometric Shapes

- **The Circle**   Traits: Bounded, repetitive, in motion
  Comforts: Habitual, pre-determined
  Danger: Living in a velvet rut

- **The Square**   Traits: Solid boundaries, balanced, equal sides
  Comforts: Protected, secure
  Danger: Little movement, little change

- **The Parabola**   Traits: Curving, growing
  Comforts: Totally free
  Danger: No mooring, fly into space

- **Polygon**   Traits: Many-sided
  Comforts: Versatile
  Dangers: Keeping track of which side is which

- **Triangle**   Traits: Definable, varied sides
  Comforts: Strong, solid, varied
  Danger: Can be too solid or imbalanced

- **Spiral**   Traits: Growing, directions inward and out-ward
  Comforts: Sense of past, and new direction
  Danger: Out of control if too fast; Regress or fall back if too slow

---

3. Risk involves transforming our ways of operating, as well as changing the "shape" of an external relationship or "object."

Sometimes we risk to broaden our repertoire; to add to our skills and abilities; to learn new ways of handling people, finances or our professional responsibilities. Sometimes we change the "shape" of our bank accounts to add to our storehouse of things, or recontour the boundary lines in a relationship, or rearrange the living room furniture.

Usually, however, we do both simultaneously, changing how we operate or behave as we change the "shape" of an asset, a relationship or an external object. By buying a car, for example, we may have to deal with, and transform, our insecurity about our future income, or our ingrained habit of frugality. Before putting our money down, we need to transform or resolve our internal mechanisms and behavior. If there is a fit, we proceed. If not, the money never gets converted into a new car. The same applies to the state of a relationship or the living room decor. For risks to be carried into the external world, we need to transform our internal ways of operating.

Even when we don't seek to change anything "outside" ourselves, but are changing "inside," it is inevitable that the internal changes are projected externally.

People in the midst of changing inside, often change their clothing styles, some furnishings, sometimes where they live, and even their life-style. One is simply a reflection of the other. The change inside — in our values, motivations, identities — is also expressed outwardly.

It works in reverse as well. When we "have to" dress up for a major occasion, we walk, talk and behave differently than if we were wearing jeans. And, it is hard to stand still wearing sneakers. Tuxedos and formal wear calm us down or at least get us to stand still.

4. Risk-taking is a skill that is learned by risking.

The practice of risk is not an academic exercise. It is not

abstract or theoretical – although understanding how the process works may be helpful in doing it well. Risking is an art form, trying again and again with brush and pallet to touch the canvas with just the right stroke and color to creatively add to the emerging picture. It involves much practice, trying our hand first at little things – as we did as children venturing into a new neighborhood, or making friends, or gambling all our marbles for the "jumbolli," the giant one with the swirling rainbow inside!

Dating gives us practice needed for mating. A summer job is preparation for a full-time one. Geometry is the precis for calculus. Learning to drive a car is the introduction to independence. Picking up our own clothes is all part of assuming responsibility for our own life.

5. **When we risk and change, we embrace the relatively unknown and thus give up a good deal of control.**

Each time the human spiral spins, it has a set of choices. It can just stop growing and go no farther. Such abrupt cessation can be caused by not knowing what to do next, or by lacking the confidence to take the next step.

A spiral can also decide to head back home, to go inward rather than out, to retrace its outlines or simply revert to an earlier revolution. Overwhelming fear usually generates such decisions to retreat.

A spiral can also pick up increased confidence in its ability to grow and complete another orbit by deciding to go on one more cycle. As it does, a spiralling line enters a new part of the page (draw one and see). In the case of a spiralling person – a living and breathing human pilgrim – he/she enters a totally new area of life. The new territory, on which a spiral has never trod before, is called the unknown.

This is scary territory. We may be motivated to go on a new expanding cycle because we have learned from past revolutions and know we have been in similar situations before. But, this particular piece of territory and this particular revolution are still new.

It is also scary because of the need to hold one's own, not fly into space or lose contact with what has already been molded in earlier orbits.

If the curve into the unknown is too fast, like a speeding car, or too wide, like a down-hill skier, one can collide, spin out of control or miss the gate. Either way, going out of control is destructive to everything already attained and to what could have been achieved.

Staying with the old pattern for fear of the unknown is lapsing into the status quo – sometimes a good tactic in the short run but hardly a model for life. Retracing one's steps may also be a temporary tactic for readjustment or problem-finding but if indulged as a continual retreat it can easily become regression. Entering an unknown, in control of your speed and trajectory, supported by the confidence of having successfully dealt with both fear and similar turns before, is an expression of willingness to enter a new cycle because you are in control of your process even though events are taking you into new space.

6. There are several segments to each turn of the spiral.

First, there is the acceptance of the challenge. Despite the fear, resistance, and the hesitation, the opportunity is dominant, the beckoning inescapable. The sense of controlling the process (although not the outcome) is reaffirmed. The opportunity is accepted.

Second, now that a new set of challenges has arrived, there is a need to destruct what already exists. The old way of doing things, the ingrained habits on a particular issue, the solidity of the bank account, the peace and serenity in the relationship, the continual streak of independence, or our normal inabilities to confront a different point of view, must be destructured.

Destructured is not the same as destroyed, for good saving habits and a willingness to build and maintain harmony in a relationship are valuable traits, to be used again. What has to be torn down is the tendency to adopt a habitual response to a situation. That pattern, that stuckness, has to be broken or destructured.

Now the third element is possible: letting in the "new" element. Now we are able to buy the new car, release some energy into moving the relationship into greater balance, include the expression of affection in our repertoire, and maybe allow ourselves to risk confronting a difference of opinion with another.

If a new way of operating can be admitted, we become eligible in *the fourth phase of the process, to reconstruct a "new creation" by using part of the old and part of the new.* Thus, we can add "spending" to our repertoire while maintaining the ability to save and buy a car for X dollars rather than 2X. The old skills are not lost, but our tendency to get stuck in them is surrendered. Our self-defeating tendency to be "johnny-one-note" even when it hurt ourselves and others, yields to a blending of old skills with the new, creating an ability to select an appropriate mix as circumstances warrant. The old pattern is broken, and now the best of both worlds can be woven together into a new, expanded and more colorful tapestry.

Fifth, as the work is completed, *we can and should celebrate the new creation.* We affirm our ability to risk and create. We display our amalgam of old and new, which is now more than the sum of the two parts. We have shown courage, persistence, and creativity, and have an expanded repertoire to prove it.

7. Risking is a creative process of "birthing," a combination of the assertive and receptive energies which exist in all of us.

Something new is created when we risk. We break out of old habits and add new skills. To do this we have to be assertive, noting what we want and taking action to attain it. We also have to be receptive, admitting new energies, skills, and combinations.

This matching and recurrence of both the masculine and feminine energies existing in everyone. The joining of the assertive and the receptive, is a creative act, creating between man and woman in biological union, a new child. In a psychological sense, our masculine and feminine energies produce children of the mind and spirit. With alternating periods of activity and rest, we can make things happen as well as let them fall into place, voicing "I want" as well as "I need," exuding direction, vitality and hard work, and at other times matching this masculine surge with the feminine insight to trust, receive and be nourished.

CHAPTER SEVEN

Process of Changing

Risking change involves both taking "a risk" as well as dealing with it. It connotes both the noun forms of a risk as a goal or area of focus, and the verb forms as well, as in "I will risk" to be involved in an ongoing process called "risking."

This chapter is devoted both to looking at risk as a goal and tracing the evolution of how that risk evolves within us as a change process.

The risk we contemplate changes with each step in the process. First it dawns on us, then we work at the various steps involved in attaining it, and then we devote energy to integrating the new creation into our lives.

This transformation of a risk from a wish to a reality is a psychological dynamic, something we experience inside ourselves as the external events in our lives are simultaneously transformed. The outer risks are both reflections and stimulants of the inner, transformative experience. We will now explore that internal experience.

To better understand our internal process around risks, it might be useful (again!) to have "a few risks" in mind while reading this material – one from the past, another dealing with a present or ongoing situation, and a third that beckons to you from the future. See the lists you generated in *Chapter Two: Self-Assessment,* and make your "selections" from them, or be spontaneous, and use any that now come to mind.

Using a code name for each – like "job," "father," "assertive," or "the bank" – can help you recall what happened inside you in the past, clarify what is happening now, and anticipate what is likely to unfold. Anchor these risks in your mind and list their code names on the next page.

Risk	Code Name or Label
Past	_Parenthood_
Present	_School_
Future	_promotion_

*   *   *

1. The Beckoning

Life goes on, and we are content or at least comfortable with things as they are. Yet, there is a gnawing sense of being something more, or at least something else. It is like a "knock" inside our heads, beckoning us not to get too settled, not to think of life as nothing but the present structure gliding into the future with only minor changes. We may not be sure we want "more" of anything, especially change, but we know deep inside there is something else to do, attain or become. We look with one eye and keep the other closed. "It is so hard, so much effort, to risk changing again, to experience our growing pains," goes the internal dialogue, "yet that gnawing sense, those little invitations, keep beckoning, encouraging me to go on one more journey."

2. Questioning

The internal beckoning does not yet need to take any particular form or focus. The feeling alone, like an internal itch, inevitably gets us to re-examine the present. We know our lives are not complete, yet we usually tend to shrug off additional work. So we let "it" go and get on with the job, the relationship, or the career.

Then that wonderful but nagging feeling returns. We take steps to improve a situation and they help, but the situation still seems incomplete. "I still want more in the relationship," "I am capable of improving my abilities," "I want and need a job with a better future," "I want to get this situation with my parents resolved," are the kinds of declarations we make to ourselves.

The beckoning now has a focus, and the adequacy of the status quo is questioned. The old structure is beginning to crack.

Figure 7.1 Steps in the Change Process.

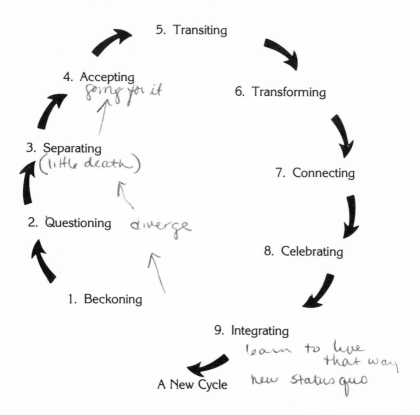

3. Separating

The increased awareness produced by our questioning, leads to the third stage, where there is a growing sense of having to surrender the old patterns and ways of operating. In separating, we start to release our attachments to "a thing or situation" as it is structured, as well as to how we handle the situation. Remember, every change involves both an external structure and an internal process. Both the situation and how we handle it have to be altered. The risk suddenly gets riskier because it means not only changing "it" or "them" but "me" as well.

The period of separating is often one of exquisite pain, an intense feeling of letting go of something formerly valued, accompanied by the delightful anticipation of eventual relief. It is both sad and happy.

And it is often lonely, for when we give up a part of our lives, it often ignites a sense of emptiness or being set adrift. Until the new "something" or "someone" emerges, we are without an anchor; the old mooring is about to disappear while the new self or connection is comparatively hazy. Frequent glimpses in the rear-view mirror yield only nostalgic reminiscing for what was or could have been. Confusion and a nagging headache usually accompany this most trying portion of the process.

4. Accepting

If the difficulties in getting through the third stage do not entice us to return and live with things as they are, then we make it to the fourth stage, accepting. Here we begin to accept the pain and the potential loss, and decide to proceed in spite of it.

We might conclude: "confronting my sister is better than living like this. To create my own space in this house, I have to start there." Or, we could decide that "taking this new job will make it tough financially for a while, but at least I will have my future back." Or the theme may center on the awareness that "giving up my freedom will not be easy and my way of life will change, but the prospects of building a relationship with X and having our own family are certainly worth it."

We move to a new plateau once we accept the need to let something go (our fear, our old job, our single status) to attain something of greater value (learning to confront our sister, starting a new career, receiving the benefits of family love). The sense of loss is now clearly complemented by a sense of opportunity. The focus becomes concrete and specific. We need to go public before God and everyone: "This is what has to be done, and this is what I am going to do!"

There is little chance now of turning back. Psychologically the old bridge is burned. We have already begun to cross to the other side, having constructed a new way of operating and thereby setting the stage for creating a new external structure as well.

5. Transiting

This stage puts us on the road to the emerging future. We have made our decision and are acting on it. We may have already taken a major risk and put ourselves on the line – confronting Sis, quitting one job to take another, or proposing marriage. Once over the watershed, we see the world differently and begin to reaffirm our belief in ourselves and in the goal we are seeking. Such risk is the first step toward having a "space" and sense of identity in your house; using your energy constructively to formulate new career goals and plans, or molding a sense of family love.

Now the windshield of the vehicle has your attention. The rear-view mirror offers only a reminder of what you decided to leave behind. Peripheral vision expands and more opportunities appear. Old negative energy is unclogged and given a positive channel. A "can do" attitude emerges.

The future is still unclear but at least it is no longer shrouded in fog. The new world has not been found but the energy is available and organized to plot the journey.

6. Transforming

Since the new bridge is built, the river can be crossed and the transformation begins. This sixth stage is especially significant for it is the first on the other side of the mountain. This is the day-to-day living out the risk to change by experiencing a resolution of the difficulties which stirred in the beckoning and doubting stages. This is the time for building on the initial act of risking with a program of activities for achieving the larger goals of self-identity, career development, a happy family life.

With a continuing plan of action, new (or re-emerging) portions of our personalities become visible. For example, the formerly shy or unsure person may become more assertive, able to say "I want" and "I need" and act on those self-affirmations.

Traveling mentally and psychologically is common during this period for it personifies the need for internal transiting of the old ways of behaving. New books, friends, contacts, skills, perspectives – all become possible and are pursued. "New" things appear on the outside while "new" ways of operating occur inside. We give ourselves increased permission to develop formerly hidden aspects of ourselves. These needs, skills and perspectives are now acted on, projected into the world, incarnated in everyday living.

7. Connecting

This welling up of the suppressed, this urge and commitment to experience ourselves and the world in new ways, inevitably brings a sense of connecting. What was initially an experiment becomes a willed experience. There is a reassurance from others. Folks respond well, cheer us on, offering what was sought without asking.

"This is it," says the pilgrim. "I feel at home here. I really like this activity. It was worth surrendering my fear of expressing anger, giving up my old job, or my single status. I like this honest relationship with my sister, this newly emerging profession, my life with my spouse and child."

This sense of connecting outside oneself is a reflection of a deeper inner connection. The external resonance both reflects and creates soundings from the depths. The gears are in sync. The tumblers click into place. A new balance and sense of harmony emerges within us, and can be projected into feelings of being at one with the new way of behaving, the new career or the growth of family love.

8. Celebrating

As the connections grow stronger, the eighth sense of celebration swells. It is not exactly Snoopy kicking up his feet while prancing down the street, but is pretty close to it. Life – or the aspect of it which has been propelling this risk cycle – takes on a generalized vitality. Life is enjoyable. It is affirmed, acknowledged, appreciated.

Celebrating is a state of being, bringing with it the perspective of the sabbath, an urge to give thanks, not wishing to change anything else for a while. It is a willingness to just *be* "for a change," throbbing with the beat of harmony and unconditional love and acceptance coming from within. It is reflected in a slower walking pace, an ability to gaze and not stare, an intensity of the senses to taste "this" pie, feel "that" touch, hear "those" birds.

More exuberant forms of celebration also emerge, like blares of a triumphant trumpet erupting from within. Statements of "I made it," resonate down the corridors. And there is an overwhelming need to be spontaneous, to fling your arms in the air and dance!

The emotions can't help but cascade, for unlike the period of doubting, we now feel full and abundant. Flashes of exaltation erupt because the continuing flow of the river cannot fully express all the new-found energy, joy, and appreciation.

9. Integrating

Integration of the old and new is en route. The sense of

ease within oneself and with the world is such that old dramas, hurts, habits and attitudes, and the old frustrations and hesitations, can be reabsorbed.

No longer do we need to keep our distance from the old ways or things, or separate ourselves from the past. All that can be reabsorbed, even embraced with dignity, as integral parts of ourselves.

Denial is no longer needed. "Owning" one's stuff, acknowledging responsibility for having been a particular way, is now possible. No blame, no shame – just acceptance and acknowledgement of the journey.

It's a mixed blessing, this sense of integration, acceptance and affirmation. Despite the knitting together of past and present and the sense of equilibrium, the body, the mind and the emotions are already preparing to embark on still another journey, another new loop of the spiral, in another area of our lives.

Each anticipated turn of the wheel produces a deeper sense that each new invitation to risk and change can be accepted with increased skill, with greater ease and confidence, with more dignity, and with a greater sense of enjoying the process.

PART II. FIGURING THINGS OUT

A Closer Look at *WHO* Will Do the Risking

Two butterflies sitting together. One says to the other, "Yes, you have changed into a butterfly now, but you still act like a caterpillar."

— Anonymous

CHAPTER EIGHT

The Journeyman

The risk taker needs to know something about where he or she is going. Yet, it is advisable for any journeyman to take stock before setting off. This self inquiry is best grouped under several headings:

1. Sense of Identity

The person who drives usually determines where the automobile goes. Backseat drivers not withstanding, the characteristics of the person behind the wheel determines the purpose, destination, and the pace of the trip.

And so the inevitable questions arise: Who am I? What is my identity? What name and rank will I use this trip?

There is a favorite story of mine. It is about one of my daughters when she was four years old. It is from another book entitled, LOVE LOOPS.

Today I went shopping for food at the local supermarket. Kris was with me. She wanted to ride in the cart, in that little pull-up shelf or basket that carts have for eggs, or bottles, or kids. So we wandered down each aisle, filling our cart with packages and cans and boxes.

I unloaded the food onto the check-out counter while the cashier started to tally the bill. She looked only at the packages, pushing them onto the mini-conveyor belt with her left hand, and then at the register which she jabbed away at with her right.

I placed the last few parcels on the counter. They were tallied, and finally the cashier looked up. Her eyes quickly surveyed the empty cart. The only "thing" in it was Kristin, still sitting in the basket with her legs dangling out the back.

The cashier blinked. Kristin smiled, slowly shaking her head. "I don't have a price," she said, "I'm a person."

The sense of identity we start with, the one we use in approaching the risk contemplated, is extremely important. If we see ourselves as a commodity then that foundation will determine the shape of the building.

If we define ourselves as having the capacity of a frog or an orangutan, that definition of self will forever minimize our projects, regardless of their worth. The name we give ourselves and the identity we assume becomes the name of our journey. Getting our identity clear first – a talented human being with untapped potential – is one of the most significant things we can do.

2. Perceptual Screens

Next, we need to check the state of our lens. Kazantkakis' story of the pickpocket who meets St. Francis and "all he sees is pockets," is instructive. Continuing the lesson, we could judge that if a shoe salesman met St. Francis, all he would see was "dusty sandals and the possibility of a sale."

The lesson is that we tend to see what we already are. We build a lens based on our identity, interests, and motivations, and we project our needs and interests onto others and into our interactions with them. Who we are becomes our perceptual screen, the guide to what attracts our attention and what we "see" and experience.

Take an example from life. A realtor, a young paper carrier and an ecologist walk down the same street. At the end of the block you ask what they saw. The responses are predictable. The realtor might notice windows in a room over a garage, which could be converted into an apartment, or a "for sale" sign on a house with stain-glass windows.

The paper carrier would probably see – as a projection of his interest and values – four houses with the rival newspaper, two houses with milk boxes (suggesting that if they already get deliveries, they might want one more!), and the fact that an elderly couple sitting on a porch are potential customers for the new edition with the larger print.

The ecologist sees the healthy elm trees, eroded soil in front of two houses with broken gutters, and stagnant water on a vacant lot.

All are right. Whose perceptual point of view you like depends on the preferences you have built, or wish to build, into your perceptual screen.

Ever notice how angry people have no difficulty "seeing" anger and getting into another argument, and that loving people keep "seeing" and attracting loving events? The question becomes, what is the state of your perceptual screens? What can you find out about your lens by monitoring what you see and hear and attract into your experience?

3. The World Doesn't Change, We Do

Remember the Mark Twain story about the fellow who at age 16 thought his father was short-sighted and out-of-it, but when he returned home three years later was astonished at how much his father had learned in so short a period of time.

The world in its entirety, all 360 degrees – everything that the realtor, paper carrier, and ecologist can see, and all the other things that all the others, with their lenses, can see as well – all of it exists, at every moment in time.

When our world view changes, our lens and aperture changes too. The shutter in our personalities stays open longer and broadens its scope to take in more. As we grow older we realize that we recognize things our parents talked about when we were young. Those "things" were always there but we were unable to see them. Now we see them because we have changed – in response to the biological and psychological clocks which increase the range and depth of our vision. We change, and with broadening ability to experience, bring more and more information, interest and values into view.

This is important for the risk-taker, because it suggests that anyone can change their experience by changing the state of their lens. Our lens grows clearer and increases in depth and breadth:

1. Every time we monitor our experiences and spot patterns.

2. Every time we become more aware of our power to create experience through our power to clean, mend, or reshape our lens.

3. Every time we make the transition from one psychological state of mind to another.

4. Every time we move to a more mature epoch of development.

The most fascinating thing about learning about lenses is that the teacher and the student are the same. The link between them is a hyphen, as in teacher-student. The hyphen is activated when we become AWARE.

Simply becoming aware of the dynamics of what we are experiencing, "to feel," in Carl Rogers words, "what we really feel," is the most profound event of all. That breakthrough allows us to become aware of the dynamics of what is really happening to us. At that point the slumbering Vesuvius comes alive.

4. Transforming Power

With an awareness and the will to enlarge your lens, you can change your experience of the world. The slice of the 360 degrees you see and absorb can be increased if you cooperate with each revolution of the cycle. You may even be able to speed it up – like the great saints and philosophers and mystics.

For most of us widening the aperture, or our growth in wisdom, depends on three factors: activating the potential of each cycle of the spiral by working on ourselves with awareness; being willing to risk and take the next step; and associating with people who encourage us to be aware, focus on personal growth, and take risks to get there.

Without awareness, the will to risk and grow, and the right company, the potential of the annual cycles will not flourish. That's why some are still childish as adults, and why some become wise even as children. It is why some see so little so late in life, and others easily learn how to see far and wide.

Again, it is the range and aperture of the lens. Watch a field mouse. Its whiskers are its source of sensory intake. A mouse knows only what it can see and feel in front of it. It may not even know there is a river five feet in front of it, as it searches for water.

Then there is the owl, which has a broader view from the tree. It sees the branches in front of it as well as the river. It also can see during daylight and at night, by sun and by moon, the symbolism being the ability to see out as well as inside oneself, a unique capacity of out-sighting and in-sighting which only humans possess. Thus, the expression, wise as an owl.

The eagle on the cliff has an even greater vantage point. It has the combined abilities or the lens of the mouse, and those of the owl, and it has more. It possesses the ability to see the entire river, and the ocean beyond and to fly to any point in the spectrum when it musters the effort, daring, trust in self, wisdom of knowing when and where to fly, and love of returning with gifts of insight.

Transforming power is what John Livingston Seagull sought and attained. He activated his ability to be a lens-maker and changed his identity, goals, and his experiences.

It is like becoming your own optometrist. Remember the last time you went for glasses and, after placing the bridge of your nose against the metal lens holder, the doctor asked if it was "better this way, or this?", "clearer this way, or this?", or "how about this versus . . . this?"

We make our selections and the world always looks and is different because of them. What is true of the physical lens is true of the psychological one as well. With glasses, however, we need an optometrist. With the human perspective, the lens-seeker also has the capacity to be the lens-maker.

CHAPTER NINE

Motivating Forces

We take risks for reasons. Behind the desire for a better job – the external factor for which we will take a risk – may be the need for financial security or for bolstering our esteem. Ten people may be seeking a better job, and are probably doing so for entirely different reasons. These reasons are called motivations.

A motivator is the motor that drives or energizes us. It is a response to needs, which accounts for our taking some actions and not others, for seeking certain things at particular times in our lives and not pursuing others. Motivation is why we invest our energies in certain directions.

Behind every outer action is a motivation. Since they are relatively unconscious, they are often difficult to detect. Clarity comes only when we start asking "why" we seek what we do, why we avoid what we avoid, or do what we do. Motivation is that set of deep-seated reasons.

We buy lunch because we are hungry. If we eat beyond the point of satisfaction, we may be satisfying a comfort need or forestalling boredom or loneliness. Eating expensive food could involve a need to impress others or bolster our mood. So "what" we do and "why" we do it can be very different things.

Abraham Maslow, the American psychologist, wrote a great deal about motivation. He disclosed that six levels of need reoccur in our lives.

The first relates to our physical needs for food, drink, sex and shelter. They are basic biological and survival needs and if we satisfy them then they no longer act as motivators. This clears the field of awareness to become increasingly attentive to our needs of security.

These are related to psychological security, the feeling of being safe and secure. Having a home may satisfy the need for

Figure 9.1 Maslow's Hierarchy of Needs.

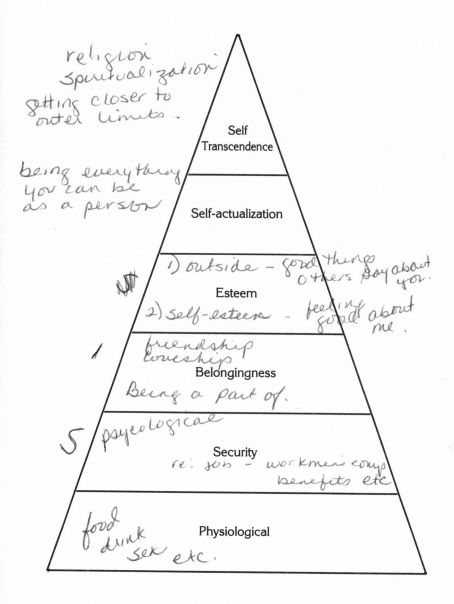

shelter, but it may not satisfy the need to feel secure and "at home" in one's house or neighborhood. If this sense of well-being is gratified, the third set of needs, love and belonging, come into view.

Belonging to a group, family, or an organization – as a valued, loved member helps satisfy this need for connections with others. We give and receive in loving contact with others. When we feel satisfied with this interchange of caring and honoring, our personalities move to the level of esteem.

The sense of esteem is the feeling of being appreciated for a way of operating which attracts praise. These "strokes" also come from inside us. We can like the way we handle a project, feel proud of our achievements, or just relax on occasion and give ourselves quiet notes of affirmation. When the sense of well-being which comes from satisfying esteem is met, the need for self-actualization is awakened or allowed to flow, because more basic needs have been satisfied and are no longer competing for motivating energy.

The best way to understand the urge for self-actualization is to reflect on what it means to be everything you can possibly be, and to make progress in developing that potential. This drive for self-actualization accounts for the successful executive wanting to play the oboe at age 55; or the retired couple who want to travel and experience the mysteries of the Orient. It is a yearning to be complete, to experience more than just well-being. It is the underlying urge for personality growth, and an expansion of insight into the appreciation of oneself and the world.

We might think that climbing this mountain of self actualization would be the pinnacle of success. But Maslow has one more need or motivator – one that consumed at least one-half of his writing but which tends to be neglected in texts on motivation and management. This is the motivation for self-transcendence.

To transcend oneself is to go beyond the limits of the earthbound ego, to explore and embrace the spiritual dimension of life. This urge may express itself through adherence to a particular religion or be reflected in a belief in and a communing with the "life-force." Self-transcendence is more than a belief in an ethical code or awareness of moral do's and don'ts. Self-transcendence refers to experiencing our spiritual nature – the birthright to be meta-human, to go beyond the ego's boundaries and this world's needs to those which transcend them and awaken a spiritual identity.

Each motivating force may occur and recur in the course of a day or week, especially at the base of the pyramid. Hunger arises at least three times a day, and issues involving security may recur periodically. The needs surrounding belonging and feeling connected with others may also be in flux, given life's changing circumstances. The need for esteem may rise and fall with the fortunes of the day. And, the motivation for actualization and transcendence, are subject to the recurring urge for quality and depth of living. Thus most of the motivators may be operating simultaneously in our lives.

Our energies, however, will tend to cluster around the lowest motivator on the hierarchy, under these circumstances:

1. When the immediate need has not been met.

If, for example, we are paddling a canoe on a glorious summer day, and our hunger bell goes off, most of us will set the paddle aside and reach for lunch. When the need below "it" on the hierarchy has been taken care of, then we are "free" again to canoe and commune.

2. When a need has consistently or frequently not been met.

In the competition for attention and energy, hunger will usually triumph over security, or security over belongingness. Only when the lower need has been satisfied consistently, over long periods, does it stop pulsating as the dominant need of the entire person, thus freeing attention and energy to pursue the next higher set of motivators.

On the other hand, the dominant theme in our lives will tend to rise on the scale under certain circumstances.

1. When the lower need is only a passing one and easily attended to.

We get hungry periodically, but if we have a steady income, we will know that such needs will easily be satisfied as they arise. Thus we need not fixate on hunger and food gathering. The fear of deprivation is not there.

Similarly the roof may leak occasionally but we may still feel secure at home and don't get stuck clinging to our mothers or houses. Our relationships may have their ups and downs, but over relatively minor issues, which do not jeopardize the loveship.

This feeling of grounding and a growing sense of having taken care of the "lower" needs may increase as the years go by, allowing us to devote more time and energy to the inner growth associated with love, esteem, self-actualization and self-transcendence.

Maslow called the lower needs "deficiency needs," things we had to provide for. He called motivators at the higher levels, "being needs," which could only be nurtured from within, cultivated with time and allowed to mature.

These dynamics become clearer when it comes to the psychological states or feelings produced when a need is satisfied. Taking care of the physiological needs usually produces a feeling of pleasure. The sense of security is likely to bring a contented feeling, and love and belongingness usually provide a glow of happiness. Joyful is the best way to describe those basking in self and other's esteem, and "fulfilled" is the internal state often associated with self-actualizing. Celebrating a sense of unity is how most people who have been "there" describe their experience of the transcendent or mystical.

The quality, intensity, and effect of these experiences are different from each other, with each providing a more complete fulfillment of the human potential than the previous one.

2. When we consciously devote our energies to the development and potential realization of a "higher" portion of ourselves.

In psychology this is known as sublimating the drive for a basic or "lower" need, such as food or sex, and willingly devoting that energy to reaching a higher state. The urge for food, sex, security or esteem, then, can through control and redirection, power greater development of our need to study, serve others, or develop our powers of actualization or transcendence.

The Hindu religion and yoga refer to this sublimated energy as the disciplined movement of the kundalini energy up the spine to the higher chakras. In fact, the seven chakras of Hinduism correspond almost exactly to the hierarchy of values described by Maslow.

Yoga is the practice of moving the kundalini, serpent, or spiritual energies of the personality from the base of the spine, where it exists in a condition of relative stupor or unawareness, through the other chakras of the body-spirit.

The next center, representing sexual energies, is based at the genitals and is akin to Maslow's physiological needs, while the third, of fire and the will to power, corresponding to Maslow's motivation of security, is near the navel. The fourth chakra of the heart (Maslow's love and belongingness) is the energy of love, aesthetics and the experience of connecting with God. The throat is the center of the fifth chakra, where the separation between oneself and God is eliminated in silence and affirmation, like the union of internal and external esteem of Maslow's self-esteem.

Maslow's self-actualization and wholeness motivator has its counterpart in the sixth chakra, the inner, mystic, or third eye, which at the center of the head, encounters the full sight and sound of God.

The top of the hierarchy in Maslow's self-transcendence is matched by the yogi seventh chakra, at the crown of the head. When the energy of life is clustered at this center, it is said that the practitioner will have achieved the ultimate point in shedding the ego, the body, and all earthly things, for the point of non-duality between the person and the universe.

*   *   *

Determining our motivation, is central to risk. It involves working with natural energies in the combined mind-body-spirit of each person and their personality. It is essential to be clear about how the contemplated risk is energized by motivation, or motivated by the real or feared deprivation in an area of need. It is crucial to know if the motivator or need is temporary and can be handled casually, or if it is a dominant theme in life.

The drive to attain a goal comes from one's center and the pool of energy available and/or channelled into that effort. Risking without support from the motivating energy is a waste of time. Risking without knowing why is futile. To know the motivator is to know the risk, for risk is the outward manifestation of the inner drive.

To achieve the risk, it is necessary to tap the available energy, or redirect existing energies from elsewhere in the mind-body-spirit system (sublimation or yogi discipline). Either way, the power and will to sustain that power are available for sustaining the risk effort.

Thus the important questions:

1. What is motivating you?

    growth change money
    status, security

2. What needs will be satisfied when you complete the risk you are currently working on?

    security, esteem

3. What drives you to take the risk you contemplate for the future?

    growth, change, money
    status, security

CHAPTER TEN

The Human Clock

Developmental psychology has made it clear that there is a sort of clock continually at work, marking time for development of the human personality. Each revolution of the clock might equal a season in the unfolding of a person's life. Each stage has a set of needs which create a lens or perspective unique to that transitional period. Thus, our view of others and the world will be strongly influenced by our interests and developmental needs.

A teenager, for example, in meeting an adult for the first time, will tend to project their interests, or in this case, developmental needs, onto that individual. The teenager might see a potential friend but also a potential parent and would, therefore, alternate between approaching and avoiding the person. At second glance, the teenager might see someone like himself who was looking for a friend to share stories about his growing independence and emerging identity.

Two-year-olds will almost dare someone to tell them what to do, for it will let them play out their developmental need to stop their dependency by setting limits and saying "No." Every age and stage is a set of such needs and viewpoints in search of an outlet. Each of these arenas is phased into, structured, and then phased out of, one wave of learnings and transitions after the other.

These psycho-social developmental periods span the approximate ages of 0-2, giving way to concerns of early childhood (2-6), childhood (7-12), teens (13-16) and early adulthood (17-21).

The adult years usually span a decade, with the last few years of each overlapping the first few years of the next (28-32), a sort of transiting out of one group of issues into another. The years in between (approximately 33-38) usually are for completing most major tasks of the epoch, before the late thirties blend with the early forties (38-42) for the renowned mid-life transition.

There are many variations within these broad periods, but generally the physical, mental and emotional changes during these epochs produce issues, concerns and ways of looking at the world which are unique to that period.

In other words, all of us are experiencing change, and feeling the risk of giving up the earlier stage for a new set of issues and beckonings that surely will have its own as yet unknown problems, growing pains and risks. The process does not change as we grow older, only the issues do.

It is a bit like Charlie Ferguson's comic report of the news on the television show, Hee-Haw. "All the news today is the same as it was yesterday," he once reported, "only it happened to different people."

Let's summarize the major issues and perspectives of each decade, remembering that these concerns are merely invitations to mature and clarify our values and identities. With each invitation there is a test. If we rise to the occasion and learn the lesson well, we lay the groundwork for the opportunities and tests of succeeding epochs. It is a big training ground for becoming a full human being.

The period of early adulthood, from 17 to 22, is filled as are all the epochs, with endings and beginnings. For many, this is the period for breaking away from old friends and values, and establishing an entre into the adult world. Going to college, or moving to one's own apartment reflect the need for greater self-identity. The prospects of marriage are further signs of the new independence as well as a growing sense of self responsibility. These primal points of purpose and direction – and all the doubts as well as vitality that youth can express in encountering new beginnings – make this period flush with both excitement and hesitation. Self-identity is so central a concern that impatience in getting there and fear of failure dominate the early adult's inner dialogue.

Thus, the period of the twenties are filled with choices: in love relationships (including marriage and a family), a job and perhaps a career; fewer but closer friendships, and formation of a more firmly-voiced value system about religion, politics and world events. The need to explore and to make the right choices is often at odds with the desire to structure success as soon as possible. Finding a balance can often be exciting but painful. Some settle this tussle with such polarities by accenting the exploration and keeping all options open, while others opt prematurely for structure and a definite plan.

It is important to remember that if we do not learn the lessons of each succeeding epoch, they are carried into the next period as unfinished business. Our work is thus compounded, for the biological-psychological clock does not stop, as an elementary school might to give us another year to complete the previous grade.

If left unresolved or filled with difficulty, the need to learn the lesson of one epoch is carried forward, potentially over-loading the system. New themes still come with the same force as if the channel were clear to work on nothing but the "new stuff." It is not unusual for many to be carrying unfinished business, like the forty-year-old who never resolved young adult lessons and is still trying to establish a separate identity from his parents.

New lessons may be learned even though earlier ones were skipped. But, wide gaps in learning can distort later issues and impede the maturation process.

Whatever baggage we carry as unfinished business, the thirties will bring its prods to development. In the thirties there is a tendency to get serious, in mood and outlook, for we think the lifestyle, values and marital and occupational choices of the twenties must be rethought, reconfirmed or changed. There is a sense of growing old – that life has to be set right with no time for fooling around.

So, if anything has to be straightened out, this is the time to do it . . . before it gets too late. Like the other periods, enough material is there to make for potential difficulties and crisis, providing the basis for reaffirming or redesigning earlier commitments.

For most, the turmoil and the need to get on with "it," is the source of the changes and the investments made in the forties. Then, we tend to establish our niches in society – in fulfilling commitments we made in our thirties to our families, jobs, or ourselves.

The forties are the decade for making it. If "it" is more a personal need to develop a particular skill, personality trait, or outlook on life, then marriage and profession may suffer. If profession is "it," others may get less attention. If all three arenas are "it," they compete for attention. The author, Daniel Levinson, says "the ladder" is critical to this decade, going up, getting firmly established, being the best at something, becoming special, having more of whatever is important than ever before.

When we are fifty, most have formed the basic structures of their lives. We may continue to rethink and perhaps tinker with the choices of the forties, but the emphasis shifts to a more caring role for others, for solid social contributions with our children and colleagues. There is increased attention to our mental and physical abilities to insure against stagnation, with increased time and attention devoted to being active, creative, "as good as I ever was." In our professions, it is no longer the "push to the top" or to be "the best" which guides us. These are tempered by the desire to contribute to others and to society. It is the age of service and mentoring.

In the sixties, we extend ourselves even more into mentoring, helping others, making time to make others happy. But, the sixties is also a reflective period when the patterns of our lives become more apparent, and we realize the meaning of the spiral, the cycles and the growing pains of each decade. There is a fullness and a savoring now, so different from the hussle of the twenties, the seriousness of the thirties, the need to make it or do that special thing in the forties, and the social inclinations of the fifties.

The seventies and eighties can also be joyful. This period of relative wisdom (assuming there is not too much unfinished business or too many lessons skipped over) also brings a growing awareness of the greatest transition of all. Increasingly, the risk and change question shifts to more ultimate concerns, such as summing up one's life and seeking the spiritual dimension, and preparing to move to a higher plane.

These transitional periods do not account for all the differences and similarities between ourselves and others, because inborn physical and mental abilities, family upbringing, and the gifts and difficulties society may provide throughout childhood and adolescence, have an enormous impact on individual personalities.

The psycho-social themes and perspectives of the developmental periods are not substitutes for such indelible imprinting of individual values, issues and ways of behaving. Yet, knowing something about our common cycles of development is important. A person at 55 is usually different in tone and perspective from someone 25 or 35. Knowing that can help establish empathy for the transitions of others, rapport with their outlook, and a sense of identity with them, for their process of struggling and celebrating with risk and change have been or will soon be ours.

This is significant, for although the unit of risk and change is usually the individual, risking and changing are interactive activities, involving and affecting many others as well.

As we implement our risk plans, it is worth remembering that the significant others affected have their own developmental needs and perspectives, and our combined processes are the same, although the specific tests may differ. Thus, we are all learning some lesson or another.

We need to realize that "our" risks may necessitate that "they" change as well. Often, unbeknown to us, "their" changes have the same design on "our" behavior. Although we may try to play the lead in our dramas — we need to remember that we are simultaneously being asked to play supporting roles in dozens of other plays, directed by people who are just as convinced that "they" are the only act in town and that "they" are the lead participants.

*   *   *

This leads to a set of summary truths. There is no other way of stating it.

1. Everyone we know or will meet is in some personal, social or professional transition. The process is universal, affecting everyone in all developmental epochs. Only the issues, perspectives, and the lessons to be learned, are different.

2. The change process for everyone is the same. It is rhythmic, with beginnings, developments, and endings – invitations to risk, to learn and to celebrate new things.

3. Our transitions have been experienced by our elders, and some day will be experienced by a new set of novitiates, some of whom will be our children.

4. The invitation to grow and learn continues until death, and is part of the ceaseless human becoming.

5. All these changes have a purpose. They are a recurring and cumulative set of opportunities enabling us to face, develop and complete our birthrights to become full beings.

CHAPTER ELEVEN

Becoming Aware

Several inter-related factors are outlined in this chapter.

1. Introspection or reflecting on our life is crucial for effective risk taking, and is the basis for making more external sources of information relevant and useful.

2. This internal or introspective information about ourselves often lies below the surface of awareness, just below the waterline of the iceberg. To reach it we need to dig a little, explore and clarify the patterns.

3. Deliberately heightening our awareness of relevant information – both internal and external – means taking periodic inventory.

4. Taking inventory of relevant information is central to our knowing *why* we need to risk, *what* we wish to attain, and *how* we will go about it.

5. Knowing something about "why, what and how" is the basis for Calculated Risk which, unlike whimsical or random risk, is both reflective and analytic.

6. There are two forms of Calculated Risk. One is proactively sought to satisfy an internal need. The other is a creative response to a situation generated by others and initially outside our control.

7. Calculated Risk – whether proactive or responsive – involves an action plan which could be either formal (written down) or informal (worked out in our heads). It guides and organizes

risk taking, for it clarifies our purpose (why), goal (what), and strategy (how).

*   *   *

1. Information About Ourselves

Several types of information are useful before and during risk-taking. Some are more important to understand our needs and to project our goals, than others. Thus a few axioms.

Of all the information available – statistical data, reports, interviews – the most significant, in the sense of reaching or touching us at our depths, is the human experience. The most significant information available to us about risk and transitions is information describing somebody's needs, wishes and situations. This data is alive and should be trusted.

Second, of all the personal, experiential and biographical information available to us, the most significant is personal experience. Trusting our feelings or needs is a crucial part of the risk process.

Third, the most important personal information available to us is contextual. It is the whole story – the entire cast of characters, our feelings, the alternatives, the options for the future – not just the bare-bones story-line of critical incidents. Contextual information is a total picture of what is and can be.

The most significant information then to consider when grappling with risk, change and transition is autobiographical, personal and contextual.

Information generated by others to describe events in which we did not participate – whether it comes in numbers, reports, analyses or interviews – can also be very important. We will refer to it, however, as it helps clarify our wishes, situation and alternatives, not as a substitute for our own testimony.

Knowing that four out of five people do something is not conclusive unless their experience is similar to ours. Knowing the statistical average doesn't help if our intuition projects a course of action above or below the average. Knowing that

Figure 11.1   The Iceberg.

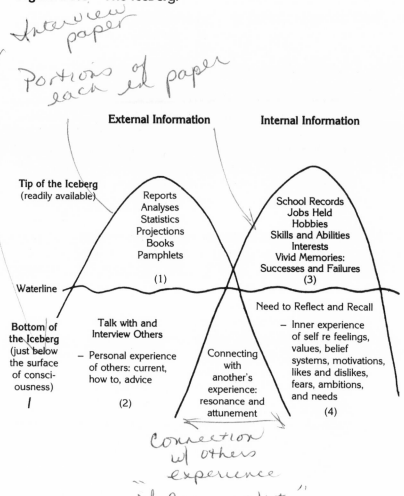

Interview paper

Portions of paper each id paper

External Information   **Internal Information**

Tip of the Iceberg
(readily available)

Reports
Analyses
Statistics
Projections
Books
Pamphlets

(1)

School Records
Jobs Held
Hobbies
Skills and Abilities
Interests
Vivid Memories:
Successes and Failures

(3)

Waterline

Need to Reflect and Recall

**Bottom of
the Iceberg**
(just below
the surface
of consci-
ousness)

Talk with and
Interview Others

– Personal experience
of others: current,
how to, advice

(2)

Connecting
with
another's
experience:
resonance and
attunement

– Inner experience
of self re feelings,
values, belief
systems, motivations,
likes and dislikes,
fears, ambitions,
and needs

(4)

Connection w/ others experience "I can relate"

three college graduates out of ten enter the computer science field should not affect us – unless computing is what we like and are good at. This internal barometer must be clarified before outside information can be useful.

External information can be helpful as we internalize it, once we see how it bears on our situation. It must be massaged by internal experience and connected with our needs, wishes, feelings. Then it becomes useful.

2. The Iceberg

There are two segments to every iceberg, the part above the water, and the part below. Information on top is readily available. The rest takes a little digging.

In our case, there are two icebergs. One deals with external information, the information that exists outside of ourselves. The other describes our internal information. Two icebergs of information, both with a portion above and a portion below the level of consciousness, make for four sources of information, or four quadrants.

The information available at the tip of the iceberg of external information comes in the form of analyses, reports, statistics, books and pamphlets (quadrant 1). Below the water-line, we have to obtain it from another through conversation or interviews (quadrant 2).

In comparison to reading a book about an area where we contemplate a risk (quadrant 1), interaction with others – since we ask the questions – should be more vivid, with a higher likelihood of being keyed directly to our interests (quadrant 2).

This also holds true in obtaining information from our experiences and inner feelings. The tip of the iceberg could include such sources as school records, work experiences, hobbies and interests, skills and abilities, or the memory of how we handled various situations (quadrant 3).

The real goldmine, however, lies within us, below the waterline. This storehouse of information contains our feelings, inner needs, past and present reactions to intense experiences. Here we find our values, belief systems, and motivations (quadrant 4).

Until all the material in quadrant 4 is brought into the open, it is not particularly useful. It may still affect our behavior in unconscious ways, but when we make sense of it, we regain control. Then we can organize and channel that information and energy directly to launching and attaining our risk.

3. Taking an Inventory

Much more information is usually available in risk-taking than we realize. It just needs to be organized and collated. That's why the periodic inventory is important, particularly when risk is pending or has already arrived.

An inventory means finding the information and putting it into useful form, which is usually determined by the questions we ask.

Let's take as an example a decision to change careers, which can be filled with many potential risks, such as our sense of self worth, our ability to expand our skills, our confidence or anxiety in assuming the financial risks to ourselves and our families, and our ability to cut the ties to the former career or job.

Taking an inventory for this potential risk includes dipping into the top of the **external** iceberg for books and materials about the career or the new company, at the top of the iceberg (1), and seeking personal and experiential information from other professionals, your financial planner, that someone down the block who did something similar last year, at the bottom of the iceberg (2).

At the iceberg of personal or **internal** information, we will probably search our memories of earlier transitions and job changes, checking to insure that we have the skills to make the transition (3).

Below the waterline on the personal side, we return to that which usually awakens the need for risk to begin with, or which is the first place we go when informed of a change coming from the outside. Our hopes and our dreams are reviewed again, and we put our fears and anxieties in perspective (4).

There may be pluses and minuses but in toto the risk of changing careers looks promising on paper (1), is encouraged by others (2), fits with our learning potential (3), and is keyed to what motivates us (4). It not only looks good (both uppers), it also feels right (both lowers)!

We are, of course, constantly in the course of updating our inventories automatically. Yet we return to them with a mission when the risk, initially beckons (or befalls us), and again when we decide and implement. Usually our explorations end up in the fourth quadrant (4), at the very spot where we initiated the search – double-checking our hopes, fears, ambitions and anxieties. Such data, although it lies below the surface of consciousness, is quickly awakened on call. We don't really "know" it until we need it, and then its guidance is available.

4. Why, What and How.

Tapping the information in the two storehouses or icebergs gives us leads, and sometimes answers, to the question of *why* are we doing something, *what* we want, and *how* will we achieve it.

It is like the points of a triangle. Point one, or *why*, discloses the reasons for our interest and possible hesitation. It provides a purpose for our subsequent inquiries and actions. Answers to "why" are found in the icebergs, particularly in the part (4) below the waterline (hopes, fears, motivations).

Point two, or *what* is the goal or risk we want to attain, is best completed after clarifying the purpose of the change, and then searching throughout the two icebergs for useful information. Slowly the goal becomes clear and is finally and officially announced to ourselves and the world.

Point three, or *how,* completes the cycle with strategies on how to achieve the goal or risk. These activities anchor

Figure 11.2

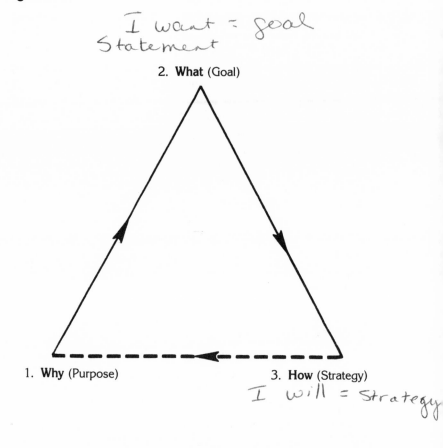

the motivation and its goal in the concrete reality of everyday life. This is the meat and potatoes. Once action is taken, our experiences are recorded, changing or altering the information already stored in the double iceberg. The gestalt is complete, and we are ready for a new focus or "why."

5. Calculated Risk

As we shall see in *Chapter 17: Styles of Operating*, there are many ways to approach and implement our risks. If the approach is one, reflective and analytic, and two, supported by concerted action, it is called "Calculated Risk."

Calculated risk is different from, and much more effective than, the other styles. "Impulsing," for example, is the tendency to act without the benefit of thinking. "Avoiding," on the other hand, is the style that thinks a great deal but never acts. And the approach of "hiding" is usually unwilling to either analyze or act.

6. Proactive and Creative Responses

Risk-taking styles which allow things to happen as they may, never taking responsibility for building motivations into concrete realities, are not proactive.

Having hopes and dreams creates a responsibility to act. Our risks and goals should grow out of us as frequently as possible. They need to be proactive, and extensions of our motivations.

When change enters our lives from outside, we have the option to simply react, or to muster a creative response. The reactive mode does not consult its information. The responsive one checks in immediately, gets grounded in its needs and desires, its skills and abilities, in an awareness of its options, and is then prepared to present a creative response.

7. Plan of Action

The process of converting what we want into reality is completed in a systematic way. We can do it in our heads, or with a notebook.

There are five parts to an action plan.

First is the statement of **Purpose.** It could read like "I need to clarify my career prospects," in a general way or keyed to a particular area. Or, we might want to clarify "how we should deal with Louie and Mildred," our mythical neighbors. A one-line statement is all we need to recognize the issue and get us started.

Our purpose may emerge from feelings stored in the lower portion of the internal iceberg, yet we must go back and check the information available in each quadrant to complete the **Inventory.**

Figure 11.3   Plan of Action.

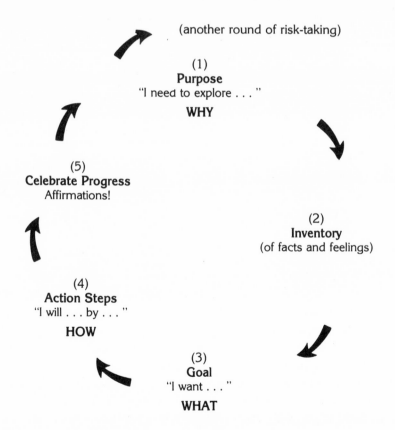

(another round of risk-taking)

(1)
Purpose
"I need to explore . . . "
WHY

(5)
Celebrate Progress
Affirmations!

(2)
Inventory
(of facts and feelings)

(4)
Action Steps
"I will . . . by . . . "
HOW

(3)
Goal
"I want . . . "
WHAT

Reviewing the inventory in our minds or notes, we look for patterns, clues, things that stand out or that "pick us out," focusing on anything telling us it is worth more time, effort and energy.

Once we have located this energy field we can generate a **Goal** statement. Something more specific and focused than the purpose. A goal reads, "I wish to become an engineer," or "I want to confront Louie and Mildred about . . . " It is best to state your intended goal in several different ways before selecting the one that will be your focus.

Getting from there to achievement involves a fourth step, breaking the goal into a set of manageable **Action Steps.** To be an engineer, we might have to "find a second job to pay the tuition," "work out ramifications with the family," and "apply for admission." An approximate timetable for each action would supply a guideline about what to do when. If we can, we might even think out the details needed to reach each step. To gain admission, for example, we might want to send for college catalogues, interview a friend who is an engineer, and read a book on the SAT exam.

As for Louie and Mildred we might need to decide whether to confront them in the middle of the night with a broomstick, or meander quietly over to the backyard fence on a sunny day.

As the action plan unfolds, it is time for the last factor: **Celebrating Progress.** We thereby affirm our goal and purpose and set a constructive tone for another round of risk-taking.

*　　*　　*

This is a mouthful, to be sure, but an important mouthful. Anyone who writes a book and simultaneously tries to get the reader to "work at" the issue in some organized way, is surely tempting fate. Yet anyone who is serious about maximizing the effectiveness of their risk and minimizing wasted energy, who in short wants to succeed and grow rather than fail and shrink, should take to heart the counsel of the last few pages.

Think about it and as you do, use the margin of this book, or that pad of paper on your desk, and make a few notes along the lines suggested. If that's still too formal or organized a pattern for you, and you have reason to trust your memory, then at least organize your thoughts in your head as you drive to work or when you have a little more time tonight or next week.

If that risk you are contemplating is really as important as you think it is, then surely it is worth some organized effort. Going into "it" unprepared, or blind, or with an impulsive itch, is not only silly, it is potentially disastrous.

If you don't believe all this now, wait until you read the next few chapters!

CHAPTER TWELVE

Involving Others

The Individual Effort

The building block for risk is the individual. We may consult with others, and act in concert with them. And, the risks we take and the changes coming into our lives involve other people.

But risk is a lonely and solitary business. It is a decision made within oneself to reach into the unknown and to gamble that the future will emerge as we wish. This gamble is difficult because when we make and act on a decision, we usually have only partial information. We don't know what is going to happen. We can minimize the risk by maximizing the information available before acting.

The calculation is completed by the individual. The individual may act as the focus for generating input from others, but collating the information and planning action rests solely with the individual.

This may present difficulties — for many prefer to lean on others occasionally and perhaps want them to make the decisions. But, individual responsibility is innately human. We are born through a social process but we are born singular, as bounded organisms, increasingly prompted from within and without, to stand by ourselves. Maturity increasingly becomes a matter of eventually taking full charge of our lives.

Risking change, then, is basically a set of actions initiated, implemented and guided by you. Even in the case of social, team or organizational decisions, it is still the individual who must assume responsibility for their efforts, will power, stamina and effectiveness.

To be fully human means having the capacity to develop a potential no other form of life has. The generic human, unlike the ape or the owl, can choose responsibility for one's actions, be aware of them, and accept the risk to choose one course of action over various alternatives.

What we are describing is an activity that is not for the birds, or for the animals, or for the insects, or for any of the other form of life. We are talking about something distinctly and innately human. In fact, through risk and change, we have the opportunity to become more fully human. Without it we would follow a pre-determined, static and limited template, being later in life the same beings we were years earlier, without further evolution.

A frog goes through the transitions of a tadpole and a young frog and then a full frog which, once it learns to croak, sit on a lily pad and catch insects, is finished with its growth cycle. A human, however, never fully completes that process. Changes continue from without and many changes are compelled from within, each of which prompts us to assume responsibility for creating our growth cycles. Individual human life, then, is potentially an ever-widening concentric cycle, and risk and change drive it.

Connecting with Others

If the individual is the hub of the wheel, then the social connections, the involving of and the impacting on others, forms the spokes. Together, both we and our significant others become key participants in acting out the dramas of the risking process.

Each participant is a bounded individual, with their own history and aspirations. We, and "they" are distinct, unique human beings. Being separate from each other, yet wanting and needing contact with others, is the central paradox of living.

Negotiating the distance between this separateness and the urge for togetherness is how life's decisions are played out. This is the stage for human growth production. The dance between these bounded entities with the "come-hither" look in their eyes, goes on twenty-four hours a day.

There are seven combinations of separateness and together-ness, each representing a point on a continuum which combines various degrees of separating and connecting energies.

Figure 12.1   The Options for Linking with Others

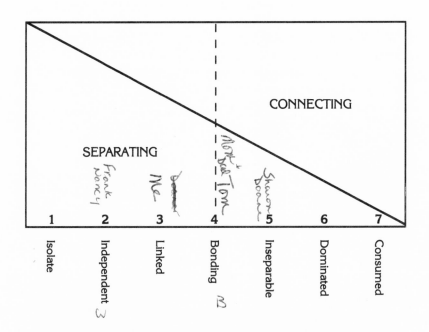

Aspects one, two and three are variations on the dominant theme of separateness. Number one, the isolate, is separate, not wanting or needing contact and certainly no ties with others. "I am here and you are there and that is how I like it," says the isolate! A graphic depiction of this extreme brand of separateness shows that "the other" hardly exists.

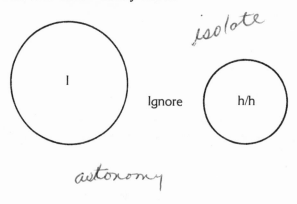

The second aspect brings the actors a little closer. One at least recognizes the existence of another, and the geographic or psychological distance depicted in number one has diminished considerably. Yet, there is still a wall around this heavily bounded and independent person and a sense that the parapet is high and strong.

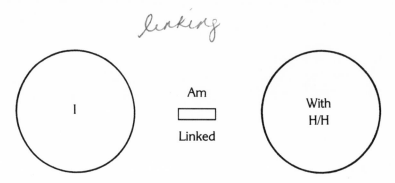

In stage three, a connection is made. Two relatively equal circles connect their boundaries with a hyphen, a potential link.

On the other side of the spectrum, beginning with number seven, we have the opposite of number one. "I" and "him" or "her" or "they" are inseparable. In fact, one contains and consumes the other. This is total dependence.

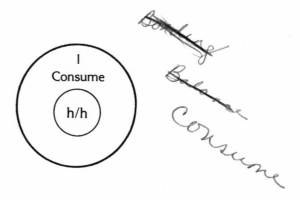

Number six is not total dependence, yet one person is still "bigger" and more controlling than the other. This is the experience of being dominated, or pushed around. It's a version of top-dog, under-dog.

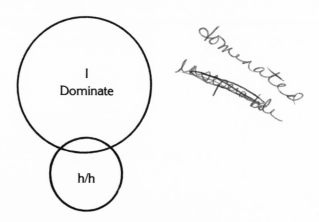

Number five edges toward a balanced middle ground and represents a strong connection between both persons through a partial overlapping of their boundaries. There is a substantive joining together, for unlike the hyphen of number three, the connection is such that they are still inseparable.

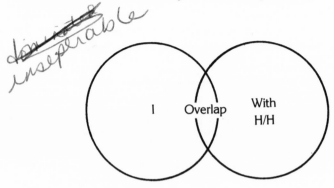

Then we have number four, the mid-point between separateness and togetherness, between the extremes of complete independence and total dependence. The boundaries are separate and distinct but now they intersect, creating at least some portion of their lives that is shared in common. The circumference of each circle is free and individual yet there is a bonding created by the bridging of the two boundaries.

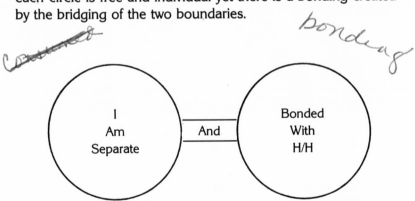

*   *   *

Obviously, the dynamic and creative tension in number four is not easy to establish or maintain, for it could gravitate in either direction. The bonded portions are not strong enough to be safe from separation. And, individuality could be jeopardized if the free waters between the two bounded individuals are compromised with too many bridges.

With all its conceivable dangers, especially if you have moved from numbers one or seven to get there – number four still has the greatest potential. In biological connections it can produce children. In the exchange of ideas, it can produce a new insight, a book, or a building. Whatever is shared in physical, mental, emotional or spiritual intimacy can generate something new, a creative bridging of the best of the two to produce a unique third entity.

This is where we, as individuals, connect with and include others who are either unwittingly involved or affected by our behavior, or who, with enthusiasm, lend us their skill and energy in support of individual or shared ambitions. This is the process of birthing by which formerly separate entities create love, families, ideas, organizations, civilizations.

Inclinations and Aspirations

There are still some crucial questions to be raised, no matter the merits or demerits of any of the options. Those questions emerge along several lines:

1. Which points on the spectrum, which of the diagrams, represent your basic inclination? Remember, we all have a right to be wherever we are on this continuum of connecting and separating – based on what we have experienced so far in life.

2. Does your dominant inclination permit variations in style or tendency, as they relate to your mate, parents, children, friends, or colleagues? It need not, but it is worth pointing out the particular variations in how you tend to operate.

3. No matter what your tendencies – in general or relative to the

various types of people you interact with – in which direction do you prefer to move, if at all? If you wish to move in a particular direction, where would you prefer to end up?

4. And, are there variations according to the kinds of interaction – like mate, parents, children – in your aspirations?

Making up our minds on all this depends on such factors as

- being honest with ourselves,
- getting clear on what we want,
- determining whom we want to associate with,
- establishing how serious we are in wanting to be productive,
- deciding on which areas of birthing most interest us, and
- finding the best combination of individuality and connectedness, one which encourages action to realize our potential to create something new.

Only when we clarify these issues, and act on our conclusions, are we able to contribute to our growth and to the development of others.

Again, note-taking can be helpful. Rethinking your past and present patterns might help clarify your tendencies and desires. Asking others about your behavior and impact never hurts. Spending some time getting clear on risks you might wish to take, and with whom, in order to bring about which creations, can be hard but exciting work.

*   *   *

The Jazz Band

There is a law which seems to operate which often takes a long time to understand. While simple, its implications are profound.

When we feel connected, linked, or in some way joined with another or share a common interest, skill, boundary or mission with them, then we feel happy. Happiness includes the sensations of feeling connected, or joined in a common effort, feeling affirmed by common bonds.

The opposite happens when we become disconnected, dis-jointed, or try to control others. Not being linked with others in a creative way usually produces sadness. This is as true in ro-mance as in career development. Linkage brings happiness. Dis-connection – through either too much independence or too much control – brings sadness and a sense of frustration and isolation.

This paradox of needing to be both partially independent and partially interdependent, through individual bonding, can be illustrated by the activities of the jazz band.

Everyone in the band knows the score of the song they are playing and how it will evolve. That score, however, is never tightly set or predetermined. And playing together never undercuts the uniqueness of individual musicians or their instruments.

In the course of a jazz band playing together, it's almost inevitable to see one player emerge from the group and play a solo. That person is in the limelight, but harmonized with and supported by the rest of the band.

Once the player has finished the solo, he or she merges back into the band, and it's time for the next musician to repeat the process. One player does not remove him/herself from social interaction, or surrender individual boundaries. The creative act is in the combination of the two processes, having the best of both – individuality, yet in concert with others.

This metaphor personifies the combination of being both an individual, and a person connected and interdependent with others. It personifies the times when we are linked with others, when the focus of that interaction changes frequently from our-selves to them. It is never "me" versus "him" or "her"; it is a successive unfolding of independence within the realm of being "us."

Our lives are sets of individual acts, but they are also lived in a social setting. Individual personalities unfold with the know-ledge and support of other kindred spirits. It's risky. It is also creative. And it certainly is growth-producing.

CHAPTER THIRTEEN

The Four Crucial Questions

Life is complex and there are so many issues, people, and needs competing for our attention. Often it is difficult to determine what it is we need and want!

The following guidelines are intended to help you sort out your priorities. They will not determine your next risk for you, since only you can make that determination. The guidelines will help you, however, to assess your strengths, focus your energies, and weigh the alternatives.

The guidelines are posed as questions since they are intended to provoke you into discovering your own answers. You should search for answers to these questions before you choose the focus of your next risk.

The Four Crucial Questions   *Start w/ Strength*

1. What are my skills and abilities, now and potentially?

Finding out what you are good at is essential if you are to use your remaining years to best advantage. Listing your talents – both those you possess as well as those for which you have potential – will enable you to play to your strengths as you anticipate your next risk.

Clarifying your abilities is also an act of self-affirmation and self-administered esteem. Feeling good about who you are and your capabilities is a dynamic which creates its own momentum. Your talents are thus more likely to be utilized and expanded.

The gathering of positive information about yourself can include a list of the skills and abilities used in the past, those you are presently using, and those you are currently developing. These inventories could include such categories as:

- **people skills** (being a good listener or negotiator);

4 • **analytic skills** (like planning, creative problem-solving, re-search, or technical analysis);

2 • **personal skills** (such as assertive, playful, loving); and

3 • **manual skills** (wood-working, pottery and the like).

Skill building is obviously a dynamic process. Our categories can change as we change focus in life, and depending on our life issues, one potential talent may get more attention than another at any given time (the arrival of children will foster the development of parenting skills, just as a promotion may activate our ability to organize or supervise).

We can and do take risks to acquire skills we do not now possess. Usually the acquisition of new skill, however, is a means to an end of a greater need; we study "X" to prepare for a better job, or we take up jogging to improve our health.

The larger risks, however, the risks which focus and develop our personal, professional and social identifies, are best focused on themes and issues which use our skills and abilities as a foundation. Why gamble with weak or shaky footings when we can enhance our cause by playing to our strengths?

Thus, before you venture out on your next risk, make an outline of your skills and abilities. In fact, it might be best to complete that list now while you are thinking of it! Use the categories of people, analytic, personal and manual skills. You could also invent your own categories. Or, you could simply make one general listing.

2. To what am I committed?

Some people have a sense for the capillary – always using their life energies on the peripheral, the inconsequential, on the issues which go only skin deep. Others possess what is usually referred to as a sense for the jugular – going instinctly to the heart of an issue, to the core, to that which will have the greatest impact.

Knowing what is of the greatest importance and what is at any given moment least consequential, is sometimes hard to discern. Issues change in their significance. Sometimes they deserve considerable attention and at other times our interest in them seems to wane.

The following exploration of the "Process of Committing" is designed to help you in several areas.

First, it will help you discern how high or low your interest is for any given issue.

Second, it will help you determine whether your interest in various issues is increasing or decreasing.

Third, it will help you determine what you are now and in the long run most committed to.

Clarity on all three points should give you clues to what now and potentially is of the greatest importance to you. Why risk growth and development on inconsequential issues from which you are withdrawing energy when you can use your risk-taking ventures to attain something of significance?

There are four steps in the process: acquainting, involving, investing, and committing. As noted in the diagram, "The Process of Committing," the four steps move in a natural progression along an "S" curve. The vertical aspect of the chart stands for psychic attention or our sense of connection with the subject. The horizontal aspect depicts the time and energy actually spent cultivating our interest in a given issue, project or person.

Risk-taking is a dynamic and evolutionary process. Thus, the use of the transitory or "ing" form for each verb. The past tense, like acquainted, or the noun form, like investment, indicate a relatively staid or static relationship to our growth.

Acquainting, then, with an "ing", is the first phase in developing an interest in a project, relationship, career, or whatever is catching your attention. This marks the first brush, the introduction, the possible beginning of something new. Our psychic attention and time we spend on the issue is still relatively low, but a new theme has entered our field of interest.

If, as a result of these initial set of contacts, either our sense of connection or the time spent in cultivating that interest increases, then the issue may enter the second area, **Involving.**

Note that the process unfolds the way a romance evolves. These ever-increasing amounts of attraction and energy

Figure 13.1   The Process of Committing.

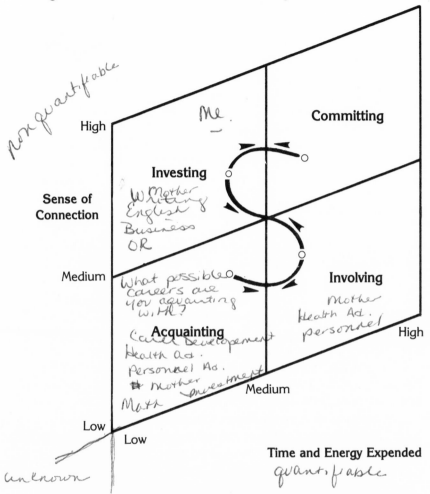

evolve as a **courtship,** and that is exactly what the process is – a person courting the object of his or her attraction, slowly getting closer and closer to uniting with it. As we move closer and closer to taking a risk and thereby embracing a new career, a new trait, or a new relationship of any sort, we literally feel the increased sense of connection with it, and focus more and more of our time and energy on it.

As the attraction continues, we move up to the level of **Investing,** and our sense of connection and the time spent cultivating that connection further increases. When we were involved, we felt the tug of attraction. When we are at the plateau of investing, we have already made a deliberate, conscious decision to devote a substantial portion of both our psychic and physical time to being with or becoming one with the person or career or trait in question.

When our sense of connection is high, and when the time and energy we devote to the object of our attention is also high, then we are at the point of **Committing.** This the highest level of union with the person or issue or project attracting us. The sense of connection is deep and usually lasting, and our calendars, anticipations, and planning start to revolve around this concern!

Risking Change at Each Level

There may be a risk entailed in letting a new issue or person enter our screen of attention. Taking that first step of **Acquainting** can be a very significant one and the amount of hesitation we feel before it may be a good indicator of the risk involved.

Hundreds of things – people, skill opportunities, jobs – can enter our flirtation or acquainting area and never proceed any further. In fact, for some of us, the risk can be to allow something to survive beyond the acquainting stage and make it to the next phase! People who are always acquainting and never or rarely advance beyond it, usually suffer from intense confusion. Nothing ever emerges as figural, nothing ignites their attention or activates their energy.

It is both exciting and scary, then, when something moves up to the **Involving** category. This is also a risky step because more time and energy are involved and a greater sense of connection is established. One can always de-escalate back to acquainting, or jettison one's interest altogether if it doesn't work out. Even that can be a difficult decision. An involving connection, once established, tends to gather momentum and is not easily diluted.

Since the number of issues entering the involving phase were fewer than those in acquainting, the same winnowing effect occurs as we move to **Investing.** Our lives are finite, as are our psychic attention, time and energy. There are an occasional few who overwhelm themselves by investing in everything; they are usually greedy, non-discriminating or both. For most of us, most of the time, however, the process acts much like a funnel: less and less is attracted into and accommodated at each progressive stage.

Committing, of course, is the biggie! If an issue is at the involving stage then it may cause you to start thinking about risk. If it is at investing, you know your sense of connection is high. But when an issue, project or person enters the committing stage, efforts to further the development of that issue are obviously worth a risk or two! Conscious, deliberate, planned efforts to protect, nurture or expand the capacities of such an issue are natural and predictable, even in the face of pain and the potential loss of something else.

The possibility of making further gains for an issue on which you are committing, is likely to out-compete anything else on your screen! Sense of connection, time, energy, you name it – this is where our devotion will be focused!

Your Inventory

It helps you to know where the issues, objects, projects and persons in your life fit in the process of committing.

First, take note of some issues or goals in your life. You might want to review and update the list you made in *Chapter Two: "Self Assessment."* To remind you of the "Arenas of Change" (Personal, Professional, and Social-Relationships), see *Chapter Three.*

Second, mentally place some of your risk-goals at the appropriate stage. With each item, note the direction it is travelling. Energy and sense of connection could be increasing or decreasing, within a given stage, or among them.

What conclusions can you draw by taking inventory? Does

it give you additional clues about where to risk next and why? Does it provide clues to what you may wish to give up and why?

3. Where Will I Make My Contribution?

Now that you have compared your goals to the stages of committing, you are in a position to face the next crucial question: based on your skills and abilities, and on your understanding of where you are in the committing process, where will you make your contribution?

The question can be put more pointedly: In exchange for the gift of life, how can you use your talents and capacity for committing, to make a special contribution to yourself and/or others?

To give, to contribute, is THE process of life: "Filling up and spilling over an endless water-fall," are from a song by Chris Williamson in "The Changer and the Changed." The system will clog if the focus is placed only on placating the temporary needs of this one, isolating ego. Life starts with a gift. It asks only for our occasional return of a contribution to sustain the process.

The best way to uncover your intended focus of service and contribution is to trust the directions indicated in both your review of talents and your map of committing energies. It also helps to complement that information by trusting your intuition and your day-dream fantasies. In your mind's eye, what do you picture yourself doing? Who are you with? What is the exchange of energy? How does the contribution take place? How are you using your talents? Which way are you moving in terms of committing?

4. Thus the fourth question: What am I willing to risk?

In its more complete form, the question would read as follows: What am I willing to surrender, to sacrifice, or risk, to channel my talents, focus my energies, and give free reign to my desire to contribute to my growth and to the development of others?

Risk entails some calculation (figuring things out ration-
ally); some grappling, mostly with our emotions, hesitations,
and fears of the unknown, and some deliberate acts of letting
go, to create space for that something new.

Without risk, our talents, our committing spirit, and our
desire to contribute, can all be for naught. If not capped by
risk, they can become ingrown. Only risk pushes us out of
the old orbit and saves us from the narrow concept of self
that is willing to develop only in the safety of the greenhouse.
Only in risk do we test our talents, focus our energies to
commit, and incarnate our urge to contribute.

*   *   *

So much for the four crucial questions. All that is left is life
and the continual task of exploring. That will take time — time for
doing things, and for absorbing their impact.

Although there probably will not be enough time to do everything we want or are capable of doing, there should be sufficient
time to do that which we consider essential. Aldous Huxley had
the right idea. It is not a matter of how much we risk, he coun-
selled, but what we learn from what we risk that makes all the
difference.

PART III. DOING SOMETHING ABOUT IT

An Exploration Of *HOW* To Take That Risk

*Knowledge doesn't keep
any better than fish.*

— **Santayana**

CHAPTER FOURTEEN

Knowing What to Do and When

When to take a risk, and how much to take, is dependent on several factors.

First, there is the nature of the change experience itself. We may succeed in controlling the range of impact of a given risk – changing one thing while trying to keep others relatively constant and the ripple-effect under control – but we still have to deal with the totality of the experience. Risk-taking is not cosmetic change. Although limited in scope, it cannot and should not be limited in depth and intensity.

Second, implicit in the process is an invitation to define oneself as an open-ended system. Risking initially involves a decision to find out who we are and where we want to go. Ultimately, we must resolve even larger issues: whether to expand our boundaries, absorb new inputs and produce new outcomes, and experience ourselves as truly open-ended and developing.

Third, the cycle of growth and development proceeds in fairly predictable ways. Knowing something about that cycle, and identifying where we are in it, is crucial to knowing when and how to initiate another risk.

These determinants of the risk-taking process can best be summarized under three headings: "The Experience of Risking," "The Self as an Open System," and "The Dynamics of the Growth Curve."

1. The Experience of Risking

Taking a risk is not just a thing or an event. It is a total experience. In involves our mind, and invokes feelings or our emotions. It stirs the spirit, raising issues of self-identity and our visions of the future. As the excitement is played out in our bodies we walk faster, breathe more rapidly, perspire, and get energized. Thus, we not only think about our desired changes but we experience their impact throughout our system. When we think of taking a risk, our stomachs also feel it, our eyes often overflow, and we grow from the inside out according to our expanding concept of self.

Risk-taking is not a head-trip but a journey of the entire personality. Our minds contain more than detached and objective thoughts. The nerve cells throughout our body, and especially in the brain, are alive with the emotions of fear and anxiety, of anticipation and courage. And, if the risk taken is in tune with our needs, we can become overwhelmed with a sense of joy and appreciation for having dared to expand our universe.

Either way, risking can and usually does produce a sense of involvement and participation in creating one's fate. Such an experience involves the entire sensorium, how we walk and talk and breathe, the look on our faces, our recollections of the past, our images of the future. Risking is an experience of creating, one that floods the entire personality, affects every aspect of its functioning, and vitalizes every part of our being.

In short, when you are in the midst of anticipating, planning, implementing or attaining any aspect of your risk-goal, you are at the point of being most alive, you are at the core, encountering the depth and breadth of your creative abilities. That sense of self as "creator" is experienced as a continuous flow of energy which uplifts and unifies your body, mind, and spirit.

2. The Self As An Open System

Any living system, if it is to grow, adapt and develop, must be or become an open system. A system is open when it has the will and ability to admit new information and perspectives, or when it has the capacity to transform itself by integrating new elements with the old, creating an amalgam superseding both. It is open when what it produces is not only creative, relevant, and usable now, but when those outcomes provoke additional inputs for the next cycle of the growth process. For a graphic depiction of the process, see Figure 14.1.

*good model
for paper.*

Figure 14.1 The Self as an Open System.

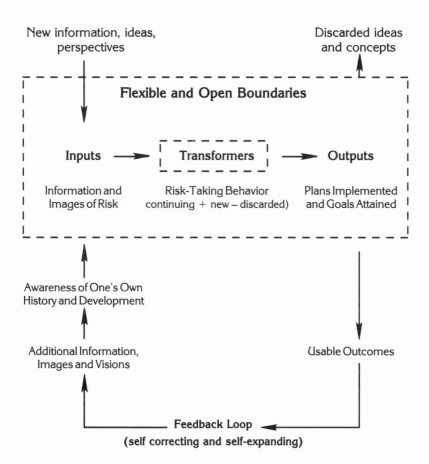

External Environment

| New information, ideas, perspectives | | Discarded ideas and concepts |

Flexible and Open Boundaries

Inputs ⟶ **Transformers** ⟶ **Outputs**

| Information and Images of Risk | Risk-Taking Behavior (continuing + new – discarded) | Plans Implemented and Goals Attained |

Awareness of One's Own History and Development

Additional Information, Images and Visions

Usable Outcomes

Feedback Loop
(self correcting and self-expanding)

With each cycle the system (person) expands and develops like a spiral: future development is based on its own sense of history, on new information, on utilizing its flexible and expandable boundaries, and on its capacity for open-ended growth into the future.

An open system is continually in process, taking as inputs those ideas, pieces of information, and perspectives the risk-taker chooses, integrating them with what already is in the system, and transforming both into the creative outcomes desired. The creations of a given cycle in the process thereby become part of the next transforming cycle since they are used by the open-ended system as new inputs into another creation.

The process tends to be self-regulating since the system produces information about the quality and usefulness of each creation and feeds that back at the point of entry for input into the next cycle. The openness of the system also facilitates a nourishing interplay between the external environment and the internal system. Whatever is available in the world-at-large can become available to us if we choose to admit its possibilities. The fund of new ideas, information, viewpoints, and vistas, for an open-ended system is, in a practical sense, almost inexhaustible. And what is no longer useful is discarded.

As we move through life then, adding the inputs and outcomes of one risk to another risk-taking cycle, we propagate our open-endedness and thus our growth and transformation. The system's boundaries have enough structure that they are identifiable and known. Those boundaries, however, are permeable – they can admit the new and release whatever is no longer functional. They are also open-ended, like the spiral, and can add cycles of growth onto itself.

Moreover, the open system is in charge of its development. It absorbs its inputs, transforms and creates what it needs, sheds the old or dysfunctional, and applies what it produces. An open system is a self-empowering system.

By being a person open to your own growth and development, you can "feed" your personality with nutrients it needs to grow and develop. Risk-taking is such a combined system. It is open. It produces creations of your choice. It provides self-regulating information through feedback. And, it is transformative in process and product.

3. The Dynamics of the Growth Curve

George Land, a writer, has devoted much time and effort to analyzing the growth and development of biological and social organisms. In his book, *Grow or Die,* and other writings, Land depicts the growth cycle as a lazy "S" curve, a concept which stimulates many ideas useful to our exploration of risk.

In looking at **Figure 14.2,** "The Risk-Taking Curve," an adaptation of Land's theory, we might see ourselves, at the present time, as somewhere in the vicinity of point "A." In terms of the "Open System," we are at the phase of Inputs again. We are aware of who we are (our self-concept), where we have been (our history), *and* have an eye for one more turn of the cycle. In short, we are entertaining the possibility of initiating another cycle or risk.

Let's assume, for the moment, that we are at the bottom of the curve (A) of the lower lip or bowl of the "S." We could feel relatively "low" for a whole set of reasons. We could have stayed too long in an unfilling job. Our enthusiasm for a particular relationship could be depleted, or we are simply tired of its repetitious routine and want to enliven it. We could also be at a relatively low ebb because fate has produced a new and unplanned-for situation; we love the new child in the house, but wish we had waited until that master's degree was completed. Or, it could be that lay-offs at work have forced us to take part-time or unfulfilling jobs. Whatever it is, we know we are not at our best. We are confused, frustrated, unsure of what to do.

This sense of having bottomed out, could generate a further downward movement (a). It could also produce a desire to move toward a more positive situation (B). Taking the more enlightened approach, we could consider the possibilities of taking a chance. Thus, we could respond creatively to the new and unwanted situation with an upbeat strategy designed to minimize the negative factors and optimize the positive ones. We could also focus on a new possibility, initiating a new set of activities designed to improve our situation. Either way, we enter risk.

Figure 14.2 The Risk-Taking Curve.

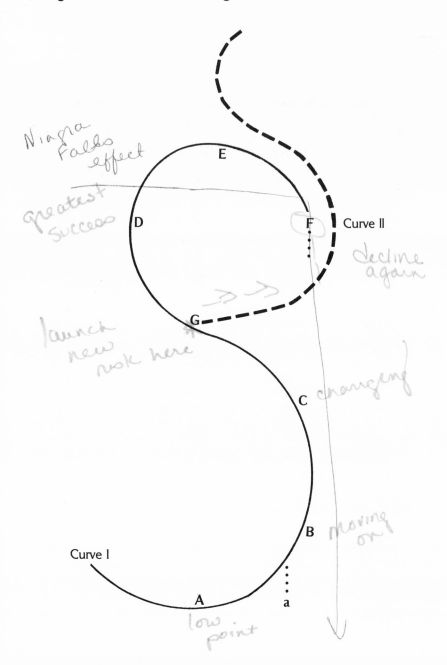

The conscious choice to change by design and thus take a chance, does not automatically get us what we want. Converting the old situation is a lot of hard work. It takes time to achieve the required mental, physical and emotional dexterity to handle a new set of circumstances.

Slowly but surely, however, we proceed up the curve of the lower bowl of the "S" curve, first at a forty-five degree angle and, with increased confidence and ability, at almost a vertical or expotential incline. At point C, we are usually feeling our druthers, activating our skills and living to our potential in a new and rapidly expanding situation.

Point D is the spot of our greatest success. It is also where our greatest possible delusion with success disguises the fact that we are riding the contours of an "S" curve. This is a dangerous time for we assume we will inherit continued success if only we continue our present behavior and pattern.

The problem with the "S" curve is that sooner or later the rate of incline will flatten out (point E). Left to its own devises, continuance of the now tried-and-true pattern will bring us into a gradual and then precipituous decline (point F).

Often, the onset of this relatively static phase will make us uneasy and thus susceptible to considering something new. A creative response to such a difficult situation would have us consider and then adopt a new transformative "S" curve, as was the case at point A. The new approach thereby becomes the launching pad for the next phase of growth.

Even if we fail to understand and anticipate the lines of the S curve, the force of events usually keeps us honest and responsive. The old ways seem and are less effective. The old products don't sell as they once did. The same routine in a relationship gradually fails to enliven either partner. And, the unchanged professional skills of yesteryear seem dramatically outmoded with each new set of college graduates.

If we persist despite the hints or the cold evidence of the need to change, if we remain blinded by memories of earlier successes, or if we become lazy, we will slide even lower (point

F) with each commitment to reverie. To hold onto the old ways or to the status quo, at this juncture, is to court disaster.

Launching a New Curve

Those who are wise and willing, will cultivate (1) their skill for diagnosing where they are in the S curve, and (2) their abilities at proactive risk. They will find a way to initiate change, take a new risk, and thereby set off a new transformative cycle. They will institute change at the point on the first S curve where they were realizing their greatest success. They will not wait for the inevitable downturn, but will get off the first curve with a new risk around point G!

This means it is best to initiate a new or second "S" curve – or curve II – not long after the point where the initial curve provides the greatest return of success. Rather than cycling down with the first curve, we would be better off launching a new one, using the ability and know-how we acquired on the first curve.

Most important, the new curve will not have a downward lip or bowl to it, as was the case at A. The new, deliberately chosen risk, initiated at G, will not be reactive but proactive. Thus, it can proactively overcome the inertia which normally sets in with end-less repetition and unexpanded ways of operating. The new risk can start faster, at a point of its own choosing, and ride the crest of the new, elongated S curve number II.

This means we have to know how and when to get off the merry-go-round near the point where things are both going well and when continuing unchanged patterns portend a serious de-cline. That is where changes, adaptations, and risk are needed to sustain new growth, which then becomes the new "S" curve.

*   *   *

These dynamics have several important messages.
1. They counsel us to leave a party while still having a good time, rather than waiting for it to wind down!

2. They counsel us to cultivate a positive attitude toward risk and to consider instituting additional changes as a matter of course.

3. They counsel us to monitor ourselves and our environment with an eye to improving things even when they are going well.

4. They counsel us to risk change when things are going poorly.

5. They counsel us not to become smug, especially when things are going well, urging us to look for new ways to activate new dimensions, attitudes, and skills.

6. They counsel us to discover new, creative methods to enliven old or continuing goals.

7. Moreover, they counsel us to think not necessarily of changing everything about our personality, profession, or relationship, but to build onto what is good, add onto what is helpful, perfect what is desired and appreciated, and complement what has already been achieved and attained. The appropriate doses of risk and change need not destroy what we wish to continue or preserve. Rather, risk and change can hone an existing skill or attitude, perfect a present relationship, and bring new life to an old job or career.

*   *   *

The dynamics of the "S" curve do not justify making radical changes as a way of staying ahead of developments. It suggests that we build on the patterns of the present situation to further perfect our ways of operating, our relationships and professional competencies. The curve of the "S" means not taking the present for granted, not assuming that things will be as successful or as exciting without continued effort, tinkering, and risking.

It suggests, moreover, that we avoid getting into grooves of endless repetition, even if the initial impact of these cycles is favorable. It suggests that we not get seduced by success or by the comfort of the velvet rut.

All things, if they are to grow, develop, and realize their potential, must give way to the constant invitation and urge to evolve. Initiating a new or second "S" curve when things are going well, and to doing so on the slope of the highest vertical rise, is the best way to insure continued growth and development.

The most important factor to note, however, is that the second curve does not do away with, or turn its back on, or fail to realize the contributions of the first "S" curve. The second one builds on the first, using it as a point of departure, insuring that its energy and accomplishments will be a foundation for the growth which follows and complements it. It is like the phases of a person's life. Each successive stage builds on and uses the best of the earlier ones. For a business, this process spells success. In relationships, it brings depth plus excitement. In our personal and professional lives, it signals the attainment of repertoire!

When we build on the past by risking in the present we obtain the future. Properly timed, premeditated change is the only way to insure growth and development of our skills, our ways of handling opportunities and problems, and our relationships and careers.

Initiating or responding to change is risky business. Estimating when to build on the first curve by initiating a new one, is not easy. Try placing your present and anticipated risks on the first "S" curve. Where are you in the cycle? What does this indicate about what you do or not do next? Do you need to take a chance, risk change, or initiate a new curve soon?

The decisive clue usually lies in a sense of prolonged repetition lacking both vitality and commitment. Having a recurring but less and less exciting, gratifying and growth-producing experience is usually the sign that we are either wallowing in the lower loop, at or near the top of the vertical rise, or already on the downturn. Unmodified continuance of the old pattern at any of these junctures, is sure to bring us to the brink of boredom, ineffectiveness, and frustration. Taking a risk, at the right time, however, can both minimize the damage and maximize the advantage!

Knowing when to change through risk can occur through rational thought as well as intuition. Whatever your way of in-sighting into a situation, trust the signal, and start thinking about building on the past with another risky modification of the present.

Risk-taking does not portend a peaceful scenario for it gives little prolonged time to rest on our laurels. It does, however, present an exciting challenge, one that is sure to encourage you to keep your walking stick available and your eye ever-watchful.

CHAPTER FIFTEEN

Character Traits

Character has a lot to do with effective risk-taking. Having a sense of presence and knowing how to proceed is independent of style, issue, and stage of development. Character is essential if we are to discover, focus and seize upon promptings for further development. The beckoning will always be there, but cutting through our resistance, setting a goal and acting on it, takes character.

Character, the measure of a person to embrace risk and change, has several dimensions.

1. Effort

To make an effort is to extend beyond one's normal boundaries. It involves a conscious focusing of time and energy on a particular issue, a willing devotion of self to the task despite hesitation and resistance.

Many authors have extolled the virtues of hard work in undertaking new venture. Scott Peck, in *The Road Less Travelled,* calls work "an extension of ourselves or moving out against inertia or laziness." The implications of effort, however, are broader than those of extending and asserting ourselves. Many of our efforts also involve withdrawing, moving away from a person or issue, minimizing characteristics such as anger or over-assertiveness, and cultivating the ability to be soft, receptive, and yielding.

Effort includes an appropriate amount of masculine energy for assertiveness or expansion, as well as feminine energy for giving, receiving and quiet acceptance. It is not uncommon today for females to seek balance in their personalities through efforts to nurture the masculine portions of themselves, and for males to nourish their ability to give and receive affection and tenderness.

Thus, effort can involve both an assertive moving toward a goal as well as a receptive letting go of a characteristic or way of operating in order to create space for a new behavior or activity. Concerted effort is essential for both, although the type of energy mustered for each is quite different.

2. Daring and the Call to Adventure

The spirit of adventure is unmistakable in risk. It involves breaking from the present pattern of behavior, and is a decision made in the face of internal hesitations and societal counsels to leave things alone. Peace, harmony and quietude – and having too much in a material way – can dull the urge to seek another growth cycle. The ability to be daring, however, urges us to be bold, brave, or heroic in the face of adversity or advise to play it safe.

Daring is a deliberate choosing not to maintain the status quo, or its equally easy opposite of taking wild gambles. Both these opposite forms of avoidance undercut timely and calculated grappling with an issue. A certain audacity is needed to cure both ills – jumping from complacency or old habits, and a calculated forging of the river of quick and dirty solutions. The search for the Holy Grail – in the face of the twin obstacles of habit and whim – is basically an adventure into one's own maturity and confidence in self.

Even Zorba the Greek, no friend of the status quo, learned to plan, think, and work out all the details in his attempts to bring logs from the mountain. When the venture did not work, he reached inside himself, with music and merriment, to re-embrace life. He supplemented whim with planned activity which, although calculated and anticipated, never reduced his ability to boldly live each moment to the fullest.

As Zorba said, " Everything in good time . . . No half measures." He recommended that when it is time to eat, we should let ourselves become the food. And when it is time to work, that we should let ourselves become the work!

On the other hand Bilbo, of Tolkien's *The Hobbit*, was no friend of change and daring. The tried, true and predictable were fine for him until Gandalf, the mercurial magician, awakened Bilbo's sense of adventure. The journey into Mirkwood, his fight with Gollum (or his darker side), his dealing with the ring of power and confronting the dragon Smaug at The Lonely Mountain, were part of renewing his urge and ability to learn through daring and going beyond his self-imposed limitations.

There are many stories, both real and mythological, that describe the urge to respond to the internal call to adventure. The testimonies of those who ventured across the seas, to the poles, into the earth, or into space, are carefully documented, from the journals of Christopher Columbus to the papers of Sir Edward Perry and astronaut Edgar Mitchell.

Daniel Boorstein's *The Discoverers*, describes breakthroughs in medicine, psychology, exploration, and technology by people who dared question the boundaries of their society and fields of inquiry. The myths of everything from "Jack and the Bean Stalk" to the "Beauty and the Beast," to Homer's *The Odyssey* and *The Divine Comedy* of Dante, to Prometheus and Osirus and Vishnu and Parzival and Black Elk – all document the unending call to adventure which has resided in every culture, of every major epoch in world history.

3. A Sense of Purpose

We take a risk purchasing goods, or in investing money. But, the risks of the person are within oneself, grappling with an inner urge to serve a larger concept of life than the mundane material factors frequently dominating it.

There is a story of a man stopping to talk to three workers on the road. He asks each what they are doing. The first answers abruptly, "I'm putting rocks in the barrel." The second replies, "I am earning a living for me and my family." The third responds with a smile, "I am helping build a great cathedral."

All are doing the same thing, but each has a different lens. One is locked into the immediate. The second relates his labor to significant but narrow concerns. Only the third has vision and sees a larger purpose.

4. Wisdom

Becoming wise means learning from our mistakes. We avoid the lure of single-loop learning, that dangerous sort of complacency which never questions the reasons behind our actions. Wisdom questions the assumptions of the previous round of decision-making, hoping to discover how the process and the goal can be improved.

Wisdom fights unquestioned repetition, reasoning that it is wise to refuse to dig an ever-deeper rut through habitual activity. Wisdom is always open to inspection and learning from mistakes. It has so much confidence that it will question earlier promises, assumptions or actions that get in the way of making the next arc of learning wider and better than the one before.

"It is not the sea that drowns you, but the puddle," Solzhenitsyn said in *The First Circle*. Hiding from the lessons of experience, perpetuating the present because it is convenient, living with exciting patterns because they have momentum, is the antithesis of wisdom. The wise wish only to call the puddle, "a puddle," and move on to deeper waters.

5. Trust

Trust is an openness and receptivity to oneself, a trusting of the message within – what I want, what I need, what I feel, what I hope for. It means less dependence on the opinions and approval of others. In the words of Carl Rogers, trust is a moving away from oughts, "away from a compelling image of what I ought to be," and "away from (just) meeting others expectations."

Trust is the willingness to be in process, to be a different set of energies each day. To paraphrase Whitman, it means

being "large, contradicting yourself (and) containing mul-
titudes."

Rogers likens the experience of trust to "being in a process of potentialities being born rather than being or becoming
one fixed goal."

6. Love

Love, to paraphrase an old adage, is "not a station in life;
it is a way of traveling." It is a process of nurturing our ability
to become complete human beings. Love also entails being
available – by assertion and receptivity – to nourish others and
their evolution.

Love is not the collapse of self, the surrender of boundaries, the depletion of one's energy. It starts with a celebration
of self, of self love, and adds to it by including others in the
radiance of one's expanding boundaries.

With love, the self is healthy and abundant. It cannot help
but contribute to another as naturally as it contributes to itself.
Love is the embodiment of stimulation, challenge, the listening
ear, the helpful arms, the hug of the body, the throb of the
heart, the resilience of the legs, the creative energy of breathing.

Love exudes and permeates by its presence. It is the
energy of the spiral. It does nothing for another but does
everything to another. It attracts by its affirmation of self. It
need not be negotiated; it just is, and both secures and permeates individual boundaries by its universality. It is infused
whenever we are willing to smile. It glows within the moment
we give thanks. It is known the world over by its spontaneous
acts of love and joy.

CHAPTER SIXTEEN

Strategies for Dealing With Risk and Change

There are several strategies we usually turn to when we sense change is en route. They apply whether we feel the change will be provoked from outside (somebody else is changing things and we need to react), or we feel the need to initiate the change ourselves.

None of the usual strategies are particularly helpful. In fact, some can be downright destructive. Sometimes we may know that, but persist anyway. See if you recognize yourself in the examples. Becoming increasingly aware of how we normally behave is essential to identifying and working out a new, more constructive strategy.

First, a review of strategies which don't work very well.

1. The Empty Stage

We think about the change — that we anticipate or wish to initiate — and let it slide. As Calvin Coolidge said of his style: "If there are ten problems coming down the road, give them time. One at the most is ever going to reach you." Unfortunately for the country the problem that did get all the way down the road was the Great Depression.

Rationalizing inaction is dangerous. Too frightened to do anything or too lazy to move, we hope the issues will take care of themselves or just go away. Consequently, we miss opportunities and get overwhelmed by our problems.

2. Always Getting Ready to Begin

This approach works hard at anticipation and planning. There is a lot of scurrying around, and a lot of furrowing of the brows, figuring out "what if" and its twin "if only." But nothing ever gets acted on. Nobody ever goes on stage and assumes responsibility for implementing anything.

Figuring it out gets all the energy, and the living out our hopes and dreams is short-circuited. "After the kids are in college," is one excuse. "One more degree," is another. "If we date for only two more years, then I'll be sure it's love," is another in this endless string of excuses, over-planning and meandering.

3. The Teenage Dance Syndrome

In this strategy, we know we want to dance and meet someone, and actually go to the dance but then stop and get bashful, frightened, self-conscious, paralyzed. We hug the wall, talking nervously with our friends or roaming around. Now it is up to the other person. Soon we reason that it took enough energy just to get there. He or she should do the work of inviting "me" to dance – make the decision, do the work, and assume the risk.

With this strategy we sometimes wait an entire evening, or in the case of adult issues, a decade or lifetime. We simply wait for someone else to do what we want to do but just don't know how.

4. Wanting It All Right Now

Accumulating information, figuring things out, having a plan, and testing it in the market place of activity, is too much for someone with this attitude. Buy that car or house, take this job, marry that person – who cares as long as you get rid of the tension of having things undecided. A bad decision is better than no decision. Never hesitate. Act!

This style obviously combines the speed and assertiveness of the tiger with the compulsive eating of the turkey. Seize and gobble. Who cares what it is or that we need time to digest what is already in the system. Decision. Decision. Decision. No forethought. No discrimination. Any and every disaster will do, as long as it's fast.

5. Over-plan, Over-control

A now-famous director of Broadway plays once asked a set designer to design and set up a few walls on stage. The walls, of various dimensions, were to serve as the backdrop of a living room. The designer thereupon built a wall which was riveted to the floor and firmly secured on all sides.

As life would have it, the action on stage the first few nights suggested that "the walls" had to be moved a foot here and a foot there. The entrance was too narrow, the hallway had to be widened, and the area near the windows expanded. The director called for the changes, but the set was so firmly secured that it could not easily be altered. And, it had been built in such a way that it was one piece; large wood pieces held the corners together rather than hinges. The set took days to dismantle, but only hours to reconstruct – this time with the "hint of a wall" using drapes, furniture, and moveable screens. The "new" scenery could be moved easily as the play progressed.

The producer's experience is instructive, for the initial instinct many have is to control all future events and the outcome of any risk. But, if we over-control and construct a plan of action which cannot be altered in the face of reality, we are wedded more to the plan and controlling people and events, than to attaining the goal the plan is supposed to serve.

If our plans called for getting to Chicago, and the best routes are via highways X and Y, and we find out later that part of highway X washed out and portions of highway Y have no food or rest stops, then it is wise to detour round the obstacles. Getting to Chicago is the important factor. How we get there has to remain flexible or our actions end up serving the need to control rather than the goal itself.

*   *   *

These strategies have something in common. They are variations on the theme of avoidance. It is avoidance of grappling with the problem for the person who never wants to go on stage, and avoidance of assuming responsibility to act for the person who is "always getting ready to begin." The perennial wall-flower is avoiding a rejection or a mistake, and the impulsive go-getter avoids figuring things out and making discriminating choices. The person addicted to control is avoiding life and the need to openly deal with its inevitable changes.

*   *   *

If we don't get caught in some form of avoidance, what are the characteristics of a constructive strategy for risk and change? What conclusions can be drawn from the examples?

There are **five essential ingredients** of a strategy which will work well and are matched with the dynamics of risk and changing situations.

1. Thought Plus Action

In initiating change or responding to one, it is essential to combine two factors: thought and action. Figuring things out, calculating pros and cons of various courses of action and their probable impacts, has to be completed first. This review of critical factors should be followed with a general action plan. That plan would clarify what we want to achieve, and what we will do – when, where, why and how – to get there. Then, we need to act. "Farming is a lot like agriculture," said Buckminister Fuller, "Only farming is doing it." Successful risk-taking involves both.

2. Flexibility

Our plans and actions must be flexible, pliable, and amenable to change. It is all in the knees, any skier will tell you. Try to negotiate a hill or mogull – whether you have anticipated them or not – with locked knees and only one plan for getting down the mountain, and you court disaster.

3. Personal Responsibility

Take responsibility for choosing. The choices include the

selection of goals or wants, as well as the means of getting there. We may have to change some details along the way, but choosing a particular direction and moving toward that goal in a rational way will minimize the risk of misdirection, fragmentation and scattering.

We can't do it all, or nothing will get done well. Priorities have to be set. Choosing includes making a decision to focus on one area and not another, or selecting and acting on a list of "to do's" and letting competing or insignificant items go unattended. In other words, choosing means letting go of a lot of other things in order to give care and attention to what has been given high priority.

4. Taking Our Time

Implementation could be modelled on the old courting process: long courtship, short engagement. Taking our time (and usually we have more than we realize, even in tense situations), gathering sufficient information, watching for patterns, comparing data to emerging needs and desires, testing tentative conclusions, and then deciding. The process initially is slow, gradual and incremental, but it picks up momentum as patterns become clear and testing and feedback warrant optimism in making the right choice.

This approach is at odds with the quick engagement, and impulsive tempo of modern society. But, making decisions about your identity, relationships and profession, involves more significant thought than ordering a hamburger. We are molding a way of life and it takes all the care and attention as we can muster.

5. Being Proactive

If you can, be proactive. Don't wait for others to make decisions for you, letting things slide until the opportunity evaporates or the problem grows explosive. Even when you are forced to respond to events not of your making, it is best to be responsive rather than simply reactive.

Responsiveness is clear on what it wants or does not want, what it is willing to do and not willing to do, and when it will compromise and when it will not. Responsive persons still maintain their sense of values and preferred ways of operating. Reacting is only a defense and lets the outside event or person set the agenda.

Some superiors, colleagues, or children will face us with narrow alternatives designed (consciously or not) to control our options and reactions, much like the parent who asks the child at dinnertime "if he wants the carrots here or there?" Sooner or later the child realizes he doesn't want carrots at all. His growing sense of identity, values, and likes and dislikes needs to speak up and set the record straight.

If nutrition is essential, and vegetables are one of the five food groups, then "broccoli, yes broccoli, is what I want," says the child. "No carrots please. Broccoli, steamed, with a little butter – that I can live with."

Carrots or no carrots is reactive only, forcing us either to yield to or rebel against a narrow set of alternatives. But broccoli represents a creative approach. It opens up the options, and is based both on reality and personal taste. Unlike carrots, broccoli is responsive!

CHAPTER SEVENTEEN

Styles of Operating

It is always fascinating to see how people deal with the large and small decisions of life. Some decisions come in the form of resolving problems – mundane, specific, concrete: what to do about allowances for the children, whether to paint the house, or to side with this client or that.

Other decisions come as opportunities: what to major in at college, where to invest money, or to take a vacation.

Still other decisions are eventually needed to resolve broader, longer-range issues, which probably involve a sizeable opportunity. The decision to pursue a particular career is one example. To get married and have children is another. And how to divide energies between personal growth and development, the family and social interaction, and professional aspirations is a third.

How we operate in the face of these issues – regardless of their significance – depends on three factors:

- our **predisposition,**
- our **ability,** and
- our **behavior or style of operating.**

Our Predispositions

Dispositions are important. They account for our basic like or dislike of risk and change. Four patterns are common. Which one best describes you?

1. To Float

These people don't look up or out very often. They do not or are not willing to look because they do not want to discover anything new, whether it is a problem or an opportunity. Their by-word is "leave well enough alone."

If these folks had the option to develop like the frog —
reach an early peak and repeat the pattern — they would take
it. Their mental encountering of the world is crab-like — their
backs protected, their eyes half-closed, the opening to the
future narrow.

This style puts the premium on peace and quiet and
tends not to recognize the possibility of an emerging self. It
doesn't seek information or new vistas. In fact, it fights external
demands to evolve or change.

Floaters tolerate making a decision once or twice in their
lives, and in so doing assume they are walking onto a conveyor
belt, where a single decision can supposedly resolve things
for the next twenty years. After that, no more decisions,
thoughts, or actions. And, of course, no more growth.

2. To Moderate

There are those people, or that approach to life or to a
particular decision, which admits new information and joys
with new activities but only within narrow limits. This approach
allows for only slight variations within the existing pattern.

The groove is so comfortable, so habitual, so soft and
womb like, that the desired range of deviation from that self-
perpetuating norm is limited. The instinctive choice is to keep
the next cycle of events from swinging far from the present
arc. The prospects for heightened awareness or attainment
of anything new and challenging is grounded by anxiety and
the fear of pain or loss.

Unlike the static connotations of the first approach, this
one may incorporate a modicum of change but only if it is
tightly regulated. Minimum change and maximum security is
the motto of the moderates.

3. To Cooperate

This approach includes the decision to cooperate with
the new and the changing, but only if the world pushes hard
enough. If one's mate is specific enough about their needs,

if the children persevere in voicing their "I want's," if that prospective new employer calls the third time, if the thrust for the decision comes from outside without our having to initiate it, then and only then, will we cooperate.

4. To Explore

This is the personality, the psychological dynamic, which deliberately and pro-actively looks for the opportunity to develop further. This is the person who willingly will ponder, anticipate, initiate, and embrace risk to create a challenge and activate untapped potential.

Our Ability to Risk

Now let's try to identify our ability to face potential change and risk.

There are three factors to examine: receptivity to opportunities, the ability to analyze information related to the potential risk, and willingness to act.

The issue of **receptivity** is related to our psychological orientation, being either open or closed to change. Openness could include being an initiator and/or being at least receptive to external prodding.

Seeking out, working with and "massaging" information we uncover are described as **analysis.** We might be inclined to investigate, analyze issues, weigh alternatives, and think out possible impacts, or we may wish to neglect the "analytic" process.

Action means willingness to act on our needs and insights, to implement activities to attain a goal, or to put energy and time into the effort.

The three factors are part of one continuum, like a thermometer or bar graph which fills up as the factors are fulfilled. Completion of the factors, then, means being open to new ideas and options, analyzing them, and taking action.

The cumulative energy amassed at the end of the four horizontal bars of energy, is one way of identifying our ability to risk. See **Figure 17.1.**

Our ability could be generalized and pervade all our risk taking, or it could be specific to particular content issues (we may, for example, be "closed" or "scared" about interpersonal issues but only "hesitant" or perhaps "willing" on political questions).

Which of the following categories best describes you – in general, or as it relates to a specific area of your life? Which category is operative now as you ponder taking a particular risk?

1. Closed

This person is obviously not receptive to change or to suggestions that it be considered. Without at least some receptivity to the idea, he/she obviously gives short shrift to analyzing information pertaining to the risk area, and certainly is not ready to do anything except maintain the status quo.

2. Scared

When we get frightened, we usually do so after a glimpse of the new. Then we back away. We hear about the job opening, meet the "girl next door," but close it off, do no investigating or homework, and let "it" drop. We consider a change but

Figure 17.1   Continuum of Energy and Ability to Risk

	Receptivity	Analysis	Action	Ability
1.	No	No	No	Closed
2.	Receptive	No	No	Scared
3.	Receptive	Analytic	No	Hesitant
4.	Receptive	Analytic	Active	Risking

retreat when it comes to thinking about and working out the options.

3. Hesitant

The blockage is on doing something about information we uncover. We may be receptive, and may even look at new information and various options, but then get paralyzed.

4. Willing

This combination of abilities describes the person who usually, or on particular issues, musters the receptivity, analysis and the action necessary to consider, develop and do something about a new idea.

*   *   *

Discovering where we are on this spectrum is not difficult. First, we can take inventory of risks we have taken or avoided in the last year or two, recalling persons, issues, things or activities which were the possible subject of risk. You might again review the list you generated in *Chapter Two,* and select a few. With each, apply the above descriptions and see which of the four levels of ability most closely describe how you behaved.

There are two sure-fire clues to knowing which combination was used when. One is the description which makes you smile when you compare it to what you did (a childlike admission, as in "Oh my gosh, that's me all right!"). The other is the refusal to recognize your behavior even though the category keeps "calling out" whenever you think of a given situation. By doing enough of these comparisons, you can start to recognize your patterns.

Styles of Risking

Our style of risk-taking is the most significant indicator of how we operate. It assumes that everyone is at least partially receptive to the idea of change, whether it comes from inside (we are attracted to or disposed to like newness and change), or from external prodding (the demands of our boss, the deteriorating condition of the roof, or the changing state of the economy).

If we assume receptivity, that leaves the crucial issues of actually using analysis and action. These two factors can be expressed in varying degrees, from little or none, to a great deal. A simple matrix of the factors and the amounts of each will yield four optional styles. See **Figure 17.2.**

The matrix can tell us something the earlier continuum could not. The continuum assumed a natural progress of energy from analysis to action, as if some do not at times devote more time to acting out an activity than thinking it out. The matrix makes it possible to affirm our right to the style of doing much or little on each dimension, mixing and matching as appropriate.

Which style describes you best?

1. The Hiding

This is the style of admitting little or no information and feeling no compulsion to move even an inch. We have a right to hide but it is not the most energizing or exciting approach. "Hiding" seems to want the world to go away, leaving us carefree and stunted in our single loop of learning.

2. The Avoiding

The option (and the behavior) of avoiding is reserved for those who think, analyze and probe continuously, and then don't follow-up. They are always getting ready to begin. "When the kids graduate, I'm . . . ," or "when the house is paid for," or "just one more graduate degree," or worse yet, "as soon as I read one more book!" are examples of the person who prepared with the best of them but is always rehearsing and never goes on stage.

3. The Impulsing

The reverse portions of avoiding produces the ingredients for "impulsing." This is action without thought, the person

Internal Risk

Figure 17.2   Styles of Risking.

Strategy - temporarily adopted
Style - 4-5 yrs

Analysis

	A little	A lot
A little	**1** Hiding	**2** Avoiding *me*
A lot	**3** *Tom* Impulsing	**4** *me* Calculated Risking

Action

intolerant of ambiguity   *Cal. Risk!*

who is out the door on one more mission before knowing what it is or where it can be found. If, the day after, the avoiding temperament moans, "if only I had!", the impulsive person with buyer's remorse groans, "if only I hadn't!"

4. Calculated Risking

When analysis and action are joined, when the benefits of thinking, weighing, analyzing, and planning are available to the skills of action and implementation, then we have the wedding of the two in "Calculated Risking."

*   *   *

Your style is obviously critical. It is the culmination and thus the reflection of your predisposition and your ability to risk. It both absorbs and consolidates the other two.

Nothing, however, is fixed or indelible about your style. If you don't like what you see, take the necessary steps to increase your capacity to analyze, act, or find a balance between the two. Calculated riskers are made, not born. They learn how by practicing . . . and then picking themselves up and practicing some more. That's the concern of our next chapter.

CHAPTER EIGHTEEN

Getting From Here to There

Whether you tend to hide, avoid, or impulse, in general or when it comes to dealing with a particular issue, you have work to do. The following are some things to keep in mind.

Everything we do is part of a training ground. The opportunities to learn how to do things for the first time or to do them better, lies in the time that you have in front of you today, this evening, this very minute. Big learnings are only elongations of smaller steps, an accumulation of tens if not hundreds of what Chesterton called "tremendous trifles."

Doing nothing is also a decision, albeit negative, to stand pat and not progress. If you get too anxious to move forward, or too self-conscious to take those invaluable little steps of incremental change, it may be best to heed the advise of the sign posted in a store in Maine, "It is better to wear out than to rust out."

On the other hand, massive change, adopted overnight, usually will be too much. The personality will be overwhelmed and traumatized, just as a hungry man's stomach will be overwhelmed if he tries to make up for six months of poor nutrition by eating too much of what would otherwise be good for him.

The change process is like the digestive process. We need to take small bites, and chew well. We need to eat only limited amounts of food at each sitting to insure proper absorption and nutrition, and to avoid indigestion, an acid stomach, and that bloated feeling.

We also need to balance the diet of change with stability and non-change. Newness needs to be supported by continuity, change by existing structure, growth by a foundation, motion by something solid beneath it. Don't try to change everything at once. Take one thing at a time, incorporate it and rest, which is what we do in pacing consumption of our meals.

Tree roots need to be firmly planted and extensive for the limbs to grow. An airplane need to be firmly structured for both stability and flexibility to fly. All sail and no anchor makes for a rudderless and chaotic journey, and is usually the quickest way to get lost. All anchor and no sail, on the other hand, keeps the sailboat at the dock. Having a little of each is the only way to get anywhere and enjoy it.

Four specific and practical tools are available to help us get "from here to there."

1. Images

Every action is first an image in our mind. Our overt activities are outward projections of our internal visions. What we do today, is a product of the cumulative images we have generated throughout life, images which are now clustered into patterns of perceiving or experiencing the world.

Our images are produced in several ways. These include the internal dialogue going on within us before and during an activity; by the images we conjure, in fear of or in positive anticipation of an experience; by images we receive or allow into ourselves as a result of what we do.

Imaging then is a way of producing information about our intentions as well as our activities. Our images before an activity are compared with those produced by the experience. Both are stored for the next thought or action in a given area.

Since imaging is the basis for what we do, we can build on this power to guide our actions by deliberately conjuring up images to create experiences we want. Imaging is the main input into creating the lens or perspective by which we view or experience the world. To borrow again from Kazantzakis, whatever we experience in meeting St. Francis will depend on the images or interest inside us, images we can project onto the unsuspecting monk.

Since images create the information and perspectives upon which we act, we can use them to guide our thoughts, rehearse efforts, support activities, and create experiences.

2. Affirmations

To affirm something is to give it positive construction. It is part of the process of baptizing an object or experience by name. Affirmation, however, deliberately leans to the positive, describing something by your preferred experience. Thereafter the name, or sentence becomes the descriptor of your experience. "That" thing out there picks up the connotations and denotations of the experience preferred in "here."

To call something "lovely," is to see it, sooner or later, as lovely, and thereafter the images of loveliness adhere to it. If it didn't already, a person or object would start to possess and reflect "loveliness." This transfer of intention to perception is as true for "courageous," "growth," "capable," or "assertive," or any affirming descriptor.

We can invest our energies in everything we experience. Affirming allows us to seize the opportunity to experience the desired images, to be attentive to them first and foremost. We are really not defining the object but merely guiding our experience. By projecting an affirming image in our labels, and sentences, or however we communicate our experiences, we can affirm the images we desire. The self-fulfilling process can propel us to become the kind of person who sees, hears, senses and creates the experience and personal attributes we seek.

Affirmations do not produce sudden transformations. Yet, they slowly but surely reinforce our belief in the descriptions used, and thereby help encourage the images and thus the behavior which will change the affirmer, thereby helping to convert the affirmation into an experience.

3. Rewards

We will need all the help we can get in making the changes we desire. That support starts with self-help, a positive attitude, with tangible rewards bolstering our efforts. To do something – even if you planned for it and wanted it – and then complain about the work involved, or the energy consumed, is to send negative incentives to your image center. But to congratulate ourselves, pat ourselves on the back, to take ourselves out for ice cream or a special treat, to celebrate a job well done, is to add positive emotional support and momentum to our efforts.

4. Applications

Whatever we do, learn to do, whatever changes we wrought, the insights and energy we used to get there, and the skills and abilities we learned in the process, are applicable not only to the particular issue in question, but to how we operate. Our personalities are a seamless web, an intricate tapestry, one part of which is affected by the color and texture of the other.

Food, for example, is nutrition for the entire body, not just the stomach! When we learn a skill, build our confidence, project positive images, affirm our sense of self, declare ourselves to be smart or interesting or effective risk-takers, we feed our entire network. Each such input is transferable to and useable throughout the organism. What is completed for "this" will apply, sooner or later, to "that." Through the process of transferability, all progress is applied throughout the system to generate cumulative and generalized momentum and mutual support.

*   *   *

We can make enormous progress in our ability to effectively handle risk and change by **applying images** which **affirm** and **reward.** The mechanisms of imaging, affirming, rewarding and applying can help us to

- weed out self-defeating behavior,
- perfect our style of or approach to risk by learning to include more analysis or action or both, and
- identify the appropriate mix or balance between analysis and action, depending on the issue.

A few illustrations help demonstrate how we can alter our behavior to perfect our styles or approach to change. References will be made to the styles 1, 2, and 3 – hiding, avoiding, and impulsing – as described in the last chapter.

For Those Who Tend to Hide (Style One)

If you tend to slough off and hide when you really want to be doing some analysis and some implementing, it is best to start by doing little things. For example, you might try the following:

1. Redo and relive, in your mind, a set of events from the past in which you wished you possessed more of the attributes of analyzing and acting. Then relive the issue and redo your behavior, doing things in your imagination which now not only make you feel good but which constructively changes the earlier outcomes. See the look on your face and the behavior you desired. Hear the words you really wanted to use and didn't until now! Allow yourself to feel what it felt like to take a chance and risk being first analytic, and then action-oriented.

2. Step back and assess what you did in your imaginative recasting of the former situation. Name the three most significant things you did to analyze the situation and three ways you acted on those calculations. See the images, hear the affirmations, and feel the rewards associated with each!

   Commit these significant "facts" to memory, or better yet, write them down! **If you can, do this exercise right now,** using the margins of this book, or separate pieces of paper to record (a) the original experience, (b) the new images of you completing both the analysis and the following actions you need and prefer, (c) the ways in which you completed both, (d) the affirmations you now feel, and (e) the rewards you received for being so analytic and action-oriented!

3. Now name the new area or issue where you want to de-

monstrate preferred behavior. Transfer the learnings (the positive images, affirmations and rewards) of step two, to the new situation. You now have the makings of a strategy, which is what you get and need when you analyze!

4. Apply the strategy to the new situation, first by imaging a set of activities you must do to handle it effectively. Make adaptations as side issues surface. Note the impacts and how you positively handle them. Test your strategy for things you may not have thought of or anticipated. Complete the picture and affirm your ability to anticipate, to be flexible, to handle the unforeseen. See or sense yourself demonstrating the characteristics you are seeking. Affirm your ability to have the impact you desire.

5. Then apply the strategy to the issue at hand, implementing the images of analyzing and acting you created.

If you learn to think and do by following your own advise, then you will eventually, evolve, with practice, from the style of "hiding" right to the style of "calculated risking." If old hesitations return or are particularly stubborn, you need to simply repeat the process and build in corrective actions.

By so using images, affirmations, rewards, and applications, you are able to

- practice in your mind first,
- guide your behavior through your desires and intentions, and
- then apply your learnings and intentions to forming the very behavior you wish in future risk-taking activities.

The approach is basically the same, whatever your style, whatever your temporary shortcomings, whatever your need for action and analysis.

For Those Who Tend To Avoid (Style Two)

For those who tend to lapse into avoidance, not acting on what needs to be done, the following are sure to help.

1. Imagine yourself going "on stage" and acting the way you prefer – much like the imaging exercise noted above.

2. Practice making little decisions throughout the day and affirming them. "I will close the refrigerator door," and observe your obvious power to do so. "I will take the dog for a walk," and reach for the leash. "I will call Louie or Mildred," and feel yourself dialing and speaking.

When you have affirmed your power to do obvious things, pick the pace up a little. Do a set of things – in the next few days – that you normally would not do but which are relatively inconsequential. This raises but minimizes risk. Again, feel your power to act and affirm your ability to act in new ways – taking a new route to work, wearing slightly different clothes, or eating with the opposite hand.

Practice first on matters of small consequence, and then on those demanding more commitment and more visibility. Slowly but surely, inch yourself toward center stage with real issues, acting on strategies you create in imaging and on your growing sense of self-affirmation.

Pace and reward yourself, and delight in your power. It is your life. You will have to live it anyway, so you might as well take charge, live it your way, and enjoy it.

Again, you are urged to try – not just read about – these suggestions. And try them now, or soon, committing your images, affirmations, rewards and specific applications to paper so you can review and repeat them any time you wish.

For Those Who Tend To Be Impulsive (Style Three)

If you are the opposite type who finds doing things relatively easy, but thinking out an issue and analyzing your options, very difficult – you have a different set of tasks to learn.

1. Practice slowing yourself down, walking slower and talking with greater deliberation.

2. Identify objects in your home or on a leisurely walk, and examine them in detail, pushing yourself to see the intricacies you normally neglect.

3. Celebrate the slowing down process and sighting the formerly unseen with affirmations of your ability to analyze, and your power to describe and discriminate.

4. If you run, learn to jog. If you bike, walk. Perfect your ability to pray (reaching out in solitude to the world's wonders) and to meditate (reaching in to quiet and celebrate your own).

5. Stop relying on your memory and don't trust your verbal banter. Write things down. Buy a notebook to be devoted exclusively to writing down ideas, solutions, and strategies to convert the present situation into the future you prefer.

6. Like the imaging exercises, see yourself as a person, with patience and deliberation, grappling with old issues and devising strategies to handle them. Transfer this approach to an issue now confronting you. Visualize pacing yourself through the steps you know are needed to move from point A to B. And most important, reward yourself in your imaging, seeing yourself enjoying your newly-emerging ability to think ahead, and implement a planned approach to crucial issues in your life.

7. Apply everything you learned in the first six steps to a set of current issues, proceeding slowly, celebrating your ability to uncover and identify factors formerly hidden. Offer thanks to the forces that energize you and receive the gifts of insight from within you.

Write your thoughts and strategies down. Walk through the old process of assessing and resolving earlier issues, and transfer that process and its lessons to the issues at hand. Above all, act with deliberation, affirming and acting on your growing ability to grapple with your issues by identifying and implementing your informed and insightful activities.

All this, and more – the rest to be created by you as you learn to trust and extend your affirmations, creations, and abilities.

*   *   *

If you have any tendencies of hiding, avoiding or impulsing, realize again that you learned those behaviors. They probably were appropriate responses to specific situations you once faced, as they may be appropriate again on some occasion in the future.

The crucial factor is not getting stuck in being a johnny one-note, the person who always uses an approach even when it does not fit the circumstances. Learning new ways of operating gives us breadth, brings us repertoire, and creates the ability to choose the best strategy for each situation.

The person who can determine which characteristic or ability to use when, is entitled to the good fortune and joys of calculated risking. He or she will also be known through the ages (or at least on his block or in her neighborhood) as the one who has grown WISE through risk-taking.

Just to make sure you get there – invest in yourself and your growing wisdom, and get yourself a new T-shirt . . . not with "Beethoven," or "Lou's Ice Cream," printed on it. The next one should have emblazoned on it your unique call of the wise, your sign or symbol or special affirmation of your effective risking. Once you have affirmed and applied your reward on the outside, then you can be sure you are learning it on the inside.

CHAPTER NINETEEN

Endings and Beginnings

There is a universal theme in the lives of human beings. Unlike the other species on this planet, humankind has the capacity to reflect on its actions, and thereby transform its personality and the world. In other words, human beings have the ability to risk and change.

To transit or make transitions is the vehicle for the growth of our personhood. To become a frog and always be a frog, however well one may croak, flip its tongue, sun on a lily-pad, plop in the water, and stretch its webbed feet, is to stay in the original limited growth cycle. "Frogness" is a single loop repeating itself, digging a repetitive groove, deeper and deeper, doing over and over what was known and perfected long before.

Getting stuck in a velvet rut is the lot of all living things except those who have the capacity to read this book. A velvet rut is nothing to complain about; even humans like its relative comfort, and often wish to stay with its grooves of peace and quietude.

Although we may occasionally want to stop our internal process and shackle ourselves with golden handcuffs – for we too grow weary of growth and development – we usually, after a look to the heavens, accept again our birthright to reflect on and perfect our lives. In the long run, we tend to attract the challenge, learn from our mistakes, and continually muster the courage to reach for ways to develop. However difficult, we do learn to overcome our resistance, work through our avoidance of the hardships involved in evolving, and cooperate with the internal engine to revolve one more time.

We are like an ever-widening concentric circle, a spiral, each turn reaching wider than the cycle before, stretching and initiating transits to unknowns, bolstered only by the awareness of having made the leap before, driven by the inner template, despite the fear, to create one more arc in our ever-expanding development.

This is the nature of the glorious beast. This is the process of becoming more fully human. This is what risk is all about. You and I are, with increased awareness, representatives of that process. Every minute, including this very one, we are in the middle of it all, heeding the call, ready to move on.

Suggested Reading

Many books will help you continue your exploration of risk and change. A few particularly insightful ones, are listed here.

1. **The Discoverers.** Daniel J. Boorstin. A history of the contributions made by a wide array of explorers, from navigators, and scientists to artists and inventors.

2. **Essays.** Ralph Waldo Emerson. A celebration of principles of human progress, and a plea for the dignity and courageousness of individual initiative in the face of social pressure or authority.

3. **The Farther Reaches of Human Nature.** Abraham Maslow. An inspiring study of human nature which analyzes the values and ways of operating which motivate us to exceed our limitations and embrace the highest orders of human behavior and insight.

4. **The First Circle.** Alexsandr I. Solzhenitsyn. The great Russian novelist, writing about the survivors of a Soviet prison camp, reminds us of how grace, dignity and fortitude can overcome any oppressor.

5. **The Hobbit.** J. R. R. Tolkien. The indominable Bilbo and his entourage of fantasy characters leave the settled life to reclaim their history and their inner and outer treasures.

6. **The Leaves of Grass.** Walt Whitman. An American epic poem that is fresh, alive, distainful, meditative, and profound, as it comments on the experience of encountering flowers, people, and the universe.

7. **The Little Prince.** Antoine de Saint-Exupery. The Little Prince leaves his tiny planet in search of a wider experience, and travels through the universe, encountering the diversity of human nature. He risks it all, learns to tame a fox, honor the stars, and reclaims his beloved flower.

8. **Love Loops.** William F. Sturner. A divorced father learns how to nurture his love for his daughters, stand on his own feet, and slowly transform his experience from one of separation to one of celebration.

9. **Man's Search for Meaning.** Viktor Frankl. A renouned psychiatrist ponders his experience as a Nazi prisoner of war, and affirms that it was the urge to create something of value that characterized the survivors.

10. **Mr. Blue.** Myles Connolly. An audacious, mystical figure who never allows rules and prescribed ways of doing things to stop his process of loving and living life to the fullest.

11. **Myths to Live By.** Joseph Campbell. An exploration of the daring actions of our ancestors and the creativity and guidance embedded in the world's mythologies.

12. **The Odyssey: A Modern Sequel.** Nikos Kazantzakis. Hailed as the greatest epic poem of the twentieth century, this sequel to Homer's narrative traces the emergence of this wanderer from the restraints of life to discovery of his freedom and his soulful love of the world.

13. **On Becoming a Person.** Carl Rogers. A classic commentary on personal growth and creativity by a psychologist who champions the individual sense of becoming with unconditional love.

14. **Religion, Values, and Peak Experiences.** Abraham Maslow. A study of the human need to create and affirm their ability

to exceed the limits of normal existence and achieve the peak human experience.

15. **Transitions.** William Bridges. Filled with insights on how to handle life's painful transitions and make new beginnings.

16. **Zorba the Greek.** Nikos Kazantzakis. A man in love with life, rebellious, kind, indominable, a man who the author says is the sort who should have lived for a thousand years.

17. Almost any standard biography or autobiography of contemporary and historical figures will include detailed accounts of how they responded to change, why they initiated change, and how they handled the risks involved in both. See, for example, books on or about Gandhi, Lincoln, Mother Theresa, Michelangelo, Freud, Martin Luther King, Eleanor Roosevelt, and Terry Fox. The list of inspiring and insightful biographies is almost endless.

*   *   *

Many authors have added immeasurably to our understanding of, and ability to, practice risk and change. Each, in a profound way, has also added greatly to the content and the tone of this book.

Some of these authors have already been mentioned, either in the text or in the "Suggested Readings." Each has produced at least one classic. A representative list of these classics follows:

Roberto Assagioli. *The Act of Will,* and *Psychosynthesis.*

Buckminster Fuller. *I Seem to Be a Verb,* and *Nine Chains to the Moon.*

Willis Harmon. *Higher Creativity.*

Nikos Kazantzakis. *Saint Francis, The Odyssey,* and *Zorba the Greek.*

Carl G. Jung. *Man and His Symbols,* and *Modern Man in Search of a Soul.*

Elisabeth Kubler-Ross. *Death: The Final Stages of Growth,* and *On Death and Dying.*

George T. Land. *Grow or Die.*

Daniel Levinson. *The Season's of a Man' Life.*

Abraham H. Maslow. *Motivation and Personality,* and *Toward a Psychology of Being.*

Rollo May. *The Courage to Create.*

M. Scott Peck. *The Road Less Travelled.*

Sidney J. Parnes. *The Magic of Your Mind.*

Frederick Perls. *Gestalt Therapy,* and *Gestalt Therapy Verbatim.*

Carl Rogers. *On Becoming a Person,* and *A Way of Being.*

J. R. R. Tolkien. *The Lord of the Rings,* and *The Hobbit.*

Allan W. Watts. *The Way of Zen.*

Ken Wilber. *The Atman Project,* and *No Boundary.*

From the Publisher

Sometimes it is difficult to finish a book like this – especially one with such an adventurous title – because there is still so much to be done!

You are obviously interested in taking a risk – or you would not have come this far. At this point, you have been introduced to the process and considered its ramifications. Your goal should now be clear and your energy focused.

Yet you now know enough about risk-taking to realize that there are still many other facets to understand. Those other facets usually revolve around three themes:

- **Oneself** – having a systematic way of clarifying your needs and your styles of operating in order to know exactly what you seek and how you can attain it.
- **The Setting** – considering features and issues that are unique to your particular setting.
- **The Organization** – understanding how to bring about change amidst the complexities of your organizational system.

In short, in order to sharpen your risk-taking abilities, you may need to learn more about either yourself, your context, and/or your organizational system. If so, what do you do next?

The author and publisher of **Risking Change** are collaborating on a set of books designed to meet the growing need for such practical, "how to" books on risk and change. Another in this series will soon be available:

Calculated Risk: Styles and Strategies of Proactive Growth, is a workbook that will enable you to test out your style on four different measures, evoke your wants and needs through reflective exercises and receptive imagery, and translate your goals into specific strategies and action programs.

*   *   *

A wide range of workshops and presentations – on the various themes of **Risking Change** – will also continue to be available through the author.

Groups who have recently sponsored such seminars and training programs with **William F. Sturner** include the Chief Executive's Program, National Institute for Higher Education, Limerick, Ireland; The National Association for Gifted Children; The National Association for Women in Banking; The Annual Creative Problem-Solving Institutes; "The International Conference on Innovation and Technology," Dublin, Ireland; the school systems of North Carolina, Nebraska, and South Dakota; Divorce Perspectives; School of Savings Banks; and The Weyerhaeuser Corporation.

For additional information, you may contact the author by writing in care of the publisher: **Bearly Limited,** 149 York Street, Buffalo, New York 14213.

□□

The world is in a
constant state of flux.

Heracleitus, ca. 540 - 480 B.C.

□□